Favorite Verse

OF

EDGAR A. GUEST

Favorite Verse

OF

EDGAR A. GUEST

I'd like to think when life is done
That I had filled a needed post,
That here and there I'd paid my fare
With more than idle talk and boast;
That I had taken gifts divine,
The breath of life and manhood fine,
And tried to use them now and then
In service for my fellow men.

—GUEST

Permabooks

14 WEST 49TH STREET, NEW YORK

Permabooks Edition, 1950
by arrangement with The Reilly & Lee Co.

PRINTED IN THE UNITED STATES OF AMERICA

TO NELLIE

*Whose devotion through the years deserves
a greater tribute*

Contents

[8]

[9]

[10]

When You Know a Fellow

When you get to know a fellow, know his joys and
    know his cares,
When you've come to understand him and the burdens
    that he bears,
When you've learned the fight he's making and the
    troubles in his way,
Then you find that he is different than you thought
    him yesterday.
You find his faults are trivial and there's not so
    much to blame
In the brother that you jeered at when you only knew
    his name.

You are quick to see the blemish in the distant
    neighbor's style,
You can point to all his errors and may sneer at
    him the while,
And your prejudices fatten and your hates more
    violent grow
As you talk about the failures of the man you do
    not know,
But when drawn a little closer, and your hands and
    shoulders touch,
You find the traits you hated really don't amount
    to much.

When you get to know a fellow, know his every
    mood and whim,
You begin to find the texture of the splendid side
    of him;
You begin to understand him, and you cease to scoff
    and sneer,
For with understanding always prejudices disappear.
You begin to find his virtues and his faults you cease
    to tell,
For you seldom hate a fellow when you know him
    very well.

When next you start in sneering and your phrases
    turn to blame,
Know more of him you censure than his business
    and his name;
For it's likely that acquaintance would your prejudice
    dispel
And you'd really come to like him if you knew him
    very well.
When you get to know a fellow and you understand
    his ways,
Then his faults won't really matter, for you'll find a
    lot to praise.

My Creed

To live as gently as I can;
To be, no matter where, a man;

To take what comes of good or ill
And cling to faith and honor still;
To do my best, and let that stand
The record of my brain and hand;
And then, should failure come to me,
Still work and hope for victory.

To have no secret place wherein
I stoop unseen to shame or sin;
To be the same when I'm alone
As when my every deed is known;
To live undaunted, unafraid
Of any step that I have made;
To be without pretense or sham
Exactly what men think I am.

To leave some simple mark behind
To keep my having lived in mind;
If enmity to aught I show,
To be an honest, generous foe,
To play my little part, nor whine
That greater honors are not mine.
This, I believe, is all I need
For my philosophy and creed.

What a Baby Costs

"How much do babies cost?" said he
The other night upon my knee;

And then I said: "They cost a lot;
A lot of watching by a cot,
A lot of sleepless hours and care,
A lot of heart-ache and despair,
A lot of fear and trying dread,
And sometimes many tears are shed
In payment for our babies small,
But every one is worth it all.

"For babies people have to pay
A heavy price from day to day—
There is no way to get one cheap.
Why, sometimes when they're fast asleep
You have to get up in the night
And go and see that they're all right.
But what they cost in constant care
And worry, does not half compare
With what they bring of joy and bliss—
You'd pay much more for just a kiss.

"Who buys a baby has to pay
A portion of the bill each day;
He has to give his time and thought
Unto the little one he's bought.
He has to stand a lot of pain
Inside his heart and not complain;
And pay with lonely days and sad
For all the happy hours he's had.
All this a baby costs, and yet
His smile is worth it all, you bet."

On Going Home for Christmas

He little knew the sorrow that was in his vacant
chair;
He never guessed they'd miss him, or he'd surely have
been there;
He couldn't see his mother or the lump that filled her
throat,
Or the tears that started falling as she read his
hasty note;
And he couldn't see his father, sitting sorrowful
and dumb,
Or he never would have written that he thought he
couldn't come.

He little knew the gladness that his presence would
have made,
And the joy it would have given, or he never would
have stayed.
He didn't know how hungry had the little mother
grown
Once again to see her baby and to claim him for
her own.
He didn't guess the meaning of his visit Christmas
Day
Or he never would have written that he couldn't get
away.

He couldn't see the fading of the cheeks that once
were pink,
And the silver in the tresses; and he didn't stop to
think

How the years are passing swiftly, and next Christ-
    mas it might be
There would be no home to visit and no mother dear
    to see.
He didn't think about it—I'll not say he didn't
    care.
He was heedless and forgetful or he'd surely have
    been there.

Are you going home for Christmas? Have you
    written you'll be there?
Going home to kiss the mother and to show her that
    you care?
Going home to greet the father in a way to make him
    glad?
If you're not I hope there'll never come a time you'll
    wish you had.
Just sit down and write a letter—it will make their
    heart strings hum
With a tune of perfect gladness—if you'll tell them
    that you'll come.

Home

It takes a heap o' livin' in a house t' make it
    home,
A heap o' sun an' shadder, an' ye sometimes have
    t' roam
Afore ye really 'preciate the things ye lef' behind,
An' hunger fer 'em somehow, with 'em allus on yer
    mind.

It don't make any differunce how rich ye get t'
    be,
How much yer chairs an' tables cost, how great yer
    luxury;
It ain't home t' ye, though it be the palace of a
    king,
Until somehow yer soul is sort o' wrapped round
    everything.

Home ain't a place that gold can buy or get up in a
    minute;
Afore it's home there's got t' be a heap o' livin'
    in it;
Within the walls there's got t' be some babies born,
    and then
Right there ye've got t' bring 'em up t' women good,
    an' men;
And gradjerly, as time goes on, ye find ye wouldn't
    part
With anything they ever used—they've grown into
    yer heart:
The old high chairs, the playthings, too, the little
    shoes they wore
Ye hoard; an' if ye could ye'd keep the thumbmarks
    on the door.

Ye've got t' weep t' make it home, ye've got t' sit an'
    sigh
An' watch beside a loved one's bed, an' know that
    Death is nigh;
An' in the stillness o' the night t' see Death's angel
    come,

An' close the eyes o' her that smiled, an' leave her
    sweet voice dumb.
Fer these are scenes that grip the heart, an' when
    yer tears are dried,
Ye find the home is dearer than it was, an' sanctified;
An' tuggin' at ye always are the pleasant memories
O' her that was an' is no more—ye can't escape from
    these.

Ye've got t' sing an' dance fer years, ye've got t' romp
    an' play,
An' learn t' love the things ye have by usin' 'em
    each day;
Even the roses 'round the porch must blossom year
    by year
Afore they 'come a part o' ye, suggestin' someone
    dear
Who used t' love 'em long ago, an' trained 'em jes'
    t' run
The way they do, so's they would get the early
    mornin' sun;
Ye've got t' love each brick an' stone from cellar
    up t' dome:
It takes a heap o' livin' in a house t' make it home.

The Path That Leads to Home

The little path that leads to home,
    That is the road for me,
I know no finer path to roam,
    With finer sights to see.

With thoroughfares the world is lined
    That lead to wonders new,
But he who treads them leaves behind
    The tender things and true.

Oh, north and south and east and west
    The crowded roadways go,
And sweating brow and weary breast
    Are all they seem to know.
And mad for pleasure some are bent,
    And some are seeking fame,
And some are sick with discontent,
    And some are bruised and lame.

Across the world the gleaming steel
    Holds out its lure for men,
But no one finds his comfort real
    Till he comes home again.
And charted lanes now line the sea
    For weary hearts to roam,
But, Oh, the finest path to me
    Is that which leads to home.

'Tis there I come to laughing eyes
    And find a welcome true;
'Tis there all care behind me lies
    And joy is ever new.
And, Oh, when every day is done
    Upon that little street,
A pair of rosy youngsters run
    To me with flying feet.

The world with myriad paths is lined
    But one alone for me,
One little road where I may find
    The charms I want to see.
Though thoroughfares majestic call
    The multitude to roam,
I would not leave, to know them all,
    The path that leads to home.

A Friend's Greeting

I'd like to be the sort of friend that you have been
    to me;
I'd like to be the help that you've been always glad
    to be;
I'd like to mean as much to you each minute of the
    day
As you have meant, old friend of mine, to me along
    the way.

I'd like to do the big things and the splendid things
    for you,
To brush the gray from out your skies and leave them
    only blue;
I'd like to say the kindly things that I so oft have
    heard,
And feel that I could rouse your soul the way that
    mine you've stirred.

I'd like to give you back the joy that you have given
    me,
Yet that were wishing you a need I hope will never
    be;
I'd like to make you feel as rich as I, who travel
    on
Undaunted in the darkest hours with you to lean
    upon.

I'm wishing at this Christmas time that I could but
    repay
A portion of the gladness that you've strewn along
    my way;
And could I have one wish this year, this only would
    it be:
I'd like to be the sort of friend that you have been
    to me.

Only a Dad

Only a dad with a tired face,
Coming home from the daily race,
Bringing little of gold or fame
To show how well he has played the game;
But glad in his heart that his own rejoice
To see him come and to hear his voice.

Only a dad with a brood of four,
One of ten million men or more
Plodding along in the daily strife,
Bearing the whips and the scorns of life,

With never a whimper of pain or hate,
For the sake of those who at home await.

Only a dad, neither rich nor proud,
Merely one of the surging crowd,
Toiling, striving from day to day,
Facing whatever may come his way,
Silent whenever the harsh condemn,
And bearing it all for the love of them.

Only a dad but he gives his all,
To smooth the way for his children small,
Doing with courage stern and grim
The deeds that his father did for him.
This is the line that for him I pen:
Only a dad, but the best of men.

Hard Knocks

I'm not the man to say that failure's sweet,
  Nor tell a chap to laugh when things go wrong;
I know it hurts to have to take defeat
  An' no one likes to lose before a throng;
It isn't very pleasant not to win
  When you have done the very best you could;
But if you're down, get up an' buckle in—
  A lickin' often does a fellow good.

I've seen some chaps who never knew their power
  Until somebody knocked 'em to the floor;

I've known men who discovered in an hour
  A courage they had never shown before.
I've seen 'em rise from failure to the top
  By doin' things they hadn't understood
Before the day disaster made 'em drop—
  A lickin' often does a fellow good.

Success is not the teacher, wise an' true,
  That gruff old failure is, remember that;
She's much too apt to make a fool of you,
  Which isn't true of blows that knock you flat.
Hard knocks are painful things an' hard to bear,
  An' most of us would dodge 'em if we could;
There's something mighty broadening in care—
  A lickin' often does a fellow good.

Results and Roses

The man who wants a garden fair,
  Or small or very big,
With flowers growing here and there,
  Must bend his back and dig.

The things are mighty few on earth
  That wishes can attain.
Whate'er we want of any worth
  We've got to work to gain.

It matters not what goal you seek
  Its secret here reposes:
You've got to dig from week to week
  To get Results or Roses.

How Do You Tackle Your Work?

How do you tackle your work each day?
  Are you scared of the job you find?
Do you grapple the task that comes your way
  With a confident, easy mind?
Do you stand right up to the work ahead
  Or fearfully pause to view it?
Do you start to toil with a sense of dread
  Or feel that you're going to do it?

You can do as much as you think you can,
  But you'll never accomplish more;
If you're afraid of yourself, young man,
  There's little for you in store.
For failure comes from the inside first,
  It's there if we only knew it,
And you can win, though you face the worst,
  If you feel that you're going to do it.

Success! It's found in the soul of you,
  And not in the realm of luck!
The world will furnish the work to do,
  But you must provide the pluck.
You can do whatever you think you can,
  It's all in the way you view it.
It's all in the start that you make, young man:
  You must feel that you're going to do it.

How do you tackle your work each day?
  With confidence clear, or dread?

What to yourself do you stop and say
    When a new task lies ahead?
What is the thought that is in your mind?
    Is fear ever running through it?
If so, just tackle the next you find
    By thinking you're going to do it.

The Epicure

I've sipped a rich man's sparkling wine,
    His silverware I've handled.
I've placed these battered legs of mine
    'Neath tables gayly candled.
I dine on rare and costly fare
    Whene'er good fortune lets me,
But there's no meal that can compare
    With those the missus gets me.

I've had your steaks three inches thick
    With all your Sam Ward trimming,
I've had the breast of milk-fed chick
    In luscious gravy swimming.
To dine in swell café or club
    But irritates and frets me;
Give me the plain and wholesome grub—
    The grub the missus gets me.

Two kiddies smiling at the board,
    The cook right at the table,

The four of us, a hungry horde,
    To beat that none is able.

A big meat pie, with flaky crust!
    'Tis then that joy besets me;
Oh, I could eat until I "bust,"
    Those meals the missus gets me.

Raisin Pie

There's a heap of pent-up goodness in the yellow
    bantam corn,
And I sort o' like to linger round a berry patch at
    morn;
Oh, the Lord has set our table with a stock o' things
    to eat
An' there's just enough o' bitter in the blend to cut
    the sweet,
But I run the whole list over, an' it seems somehow
    that I
Find the keenest sort o' pleasure in a chunk o' raisin
    pie.

There are pies that start the water circulatin' in the
    mouth;
There are pies that wear the flavor of the warm an'
    sunny south;
Some with oriental spices spur the drowsy appe-
    tite
An' just fill a fellow's being with a thrill o' real
    delight;

But for downright solid goodness that comes drippin'
    from the sky
There is nothing quite the equal of a chunk o' raisin
    pie.

I'm admittin' tastes are diff'runt, I'm not settin' up
    myself
As the judge an' final critic of the good things on
    the shelf.
I'm just sort o' payin' tribute to a simple joy on
    earth,
Sort o' feebly testifyin' to its lasting charm an'
    worth,
An' I'll hold to this conclusion till it comes my time
    to die,
That there's no dessert that's finer than a chunk o'
    raisin pie.

Be a Friend

Be a friend. You don't need money:
Just a disposition sunny;
Just the wish to help another
Get along some way or other;
Just a kindly hand extended
Out to one who's unbefriended;
Just the will to give or lend,
This will make you someone's friend.

Be a friend. You don't need glory.
Friendship is a simple story.

Pass by trifling errors blindly,
Gaze on honest effort kindly,
Cheer the youth who's bravely trying,
Pity him who's sadly sighing;
Just a little labor spend
On the duties of a friend.

Be a friend. The pay is bigger
(Though not written by a figure)
Than is earned by people clever
In what's merely self-endeavor.
You'll have friends instead of neighbors
For the profits of your labors;
You'll be richer in the end
Than a prince, if you're a friend.

The Man Who Couldn't Save

He spent what he made, or he gave it away,
Tried to save money, and would for a day,
Started a bank-account time an' again,
Got a hundred or so for a nest egg, an' then
Some fellow that needed it more than he did,
Who was down on his luck, with a sick wife or kid,
Came along an' he wasted no time till he went
An' drew out the coin that for saving was meant.

They say he died poor, and I guess that is so:
To pile up a fortune he hadn't a show;
He worked all the time and good money he made,
Was known as an excellent man at his trade,

But he saw too much, heard too much, felt too much
     here
To save anything by the end of the year,
An' the shabbiest wreck the Lord ever let live
Could get money from him if he had it to give.

I've seen him slip dimes to the bums on the street
Who told him they hungered for something to eat,
An' though I remarked they were going for drink
He'd say: "Mebbe so. But I'd just hate to think
That fellow was hungry an' I'd passed him by;
I'd rather be fooled twenty times by a lie
Than wonder if one of 'em I wouldn't feed
Had told me the truth an' was really in need."

Never stinted his family out of a thing:
They had everything that his money could bring;
Said he'd rather be broke and just know they were
     glad,
Than rich, with them pining an' wishing they had
Some of the pleasures his money would buy;
Said he never could look a bank book in the eye
If he knew it had grown on the pleasures and joys
That he'd robbed from his wife and his girls and his
     boys.

Queer sort of notion he had, I confess,
Yet many a rich man on earth is mourned less.
All who had known him came back to his side
To honor his name on the day that he died,

Didn't leave much in the bank, it is true,
But did leave a fortune in people who knew
The big heart of him, an' I'm willing to swear
That to-day he is one of the richest up there.

At the Door

He wiped his shoes before his door,
But ere he entered he did more:
'Twas not enough to cleanse his feet
Of dirt they'd gathered in the street;
He stood and dusted off his mind
And left all trace of care behind.
"In here I will not take," said he,
"The stains the day has brought to me.
"Beyond this door shall never go
The burdens that are mine to know;
The day is done, and here I leave
The petty things that vex and grieve;
What clings to me of hate and sin
To them I will not carry in;
Only the good shall go with me
For their devoted eyes to see.

"I will not burden them with cares,
Nor track the home with grim affairs;
I will not at my table sit
With soul unclean, and mind unfit;
Beyond this door I will not take
The outward signs of inward ache;

I will not take a dreary mind
Into this house for them to find."

He wiped his shoes before his door,
But paused to do a little more.
He dusted off the stains of strife,
The mud that's incident to life,
The blemishes of careless thought,
The traces of the fight he'd fought,
The selfish humors and the mean,
And when he entered he was clean.

Duty

To do your little bit of toil,
   To play life's game with head erect;
To stoop to nothing that would soil
   Your honor or your self-respect;
To win what gold and fame you can,
But first of all to be a man.

To know the bitter and the sweet,
   The sunshine and the days of rain;
To meet both victory and defeat,
   Nor boast too loudly nor complain;
To face whatever fates befall
And be a man throughout it all.

To seek success in honest strife,
   But not to value it so much

That, winning it, you go through life
    Stained by dishonor's scarlet touch.
What goal or dream you choose, pursue,
But be a man whate'er you do!

When Father Shook the Stove

'Twas not so many years ago,
    Say, twenty-two or three,
When zero weather or below
    Held many a thrill for me.
Then in my icy room I slept
    A youngster's sweet repose,
And always on my form I kept
    My flannel underclothes.
Then I was roused by sudden shock
    Though still to sleep I strove,
I knew that it was seven o'clock
    When father shook the stove.

I never heard him quit his bed
    Or his alarm clock ring;
I never heard his gentle tread,
    Or his attempts to sing;
The sun that found my window pane
    On me was wholly lost,
Though many a sunbeam tried in vain
    To penetrate the frost.

To human voice I never stirred,
  But deeper down I dove
Beneath the covers, when I heard
  My father shake the stove.

To-day it all comes back to me
  And I can hear it still;
He seemed to take a special glee
  In shaking with a will.
He flung the noisy dampers back,
  Then rattled steel on steel,
Until the force of his attack
  The building seemed to feel.
Though I'd a youngster's heavy eyes
  All sleep from them he drove;
It seemed to me the dead must rise
  When father shook the stove.

Now radiators thump and pound
  And every room is warm,
And modern men new ways have **found**
  To shield us from the storm.
The window panes are seldom glossed
  The way they used to be;
The pictures left by old Jack Frost
  Our children never see.
And now that he has gone to rest
  In God's great slumber grove,
I often think those days were best
  When father shook the stove.

The Junk Box

My father often used to say:
"My boy don't throw a thing away:
You'll find a use for it some day."

So in a box he stored up things,
Bent nails, old washers, pipes and rings,
And bolts and nuts and rusty springs.

Despite each blemish and each flaw,
Some use for everything he saw;
With things material, this was law.

And often when he'd work to do,
He searched the junk box through and through
And found old stuff as good as new.

And I have often thought since then,
That father did the same with men;
He knew he'd need their help again.

It seems to me he understood
That men, as well as iron and wood,
May broken be and still be good.

Despite the vices he'd display
He never threw a man away,
But kept him for another day.

A human junk box is this earth
And into it we're tossed at birth,
To wait the day we'll be of worth.

Though bent and twisted, weak of will,
And full of flaws and lacking skill,
Some service each can render still.

Sacrifice

When he has more than he can eat
To feed a stranger's not a feat.

When he has more than he can spend
It isn't hard to give or lend.

Who gives but what he'll never miss
Will never know what giving is.

He'll win few praises from his Lord
Who does but what he can afford.

The widow's mite to heaven went
Because real sacrifice it meant.

See It Through

When you're up against a trouble,
    Meet it squarely, face to face;
Lift your chin and set your shoulders,
    Plant your feet and take a brace.
When it's vain to try to dodge it,
    Do the best that you can do;
You may fail, but you may conquer,
    See it through!

Black may be the clouds about you
　　And your future may seem grim,
But don't let your nerve desert you;
　　Keep yourself in fighting trim.
If the worst is bound to happen,
　　Spite of all that you can do,
Running from it will not save you,
　　See it through!

Even hope may seem but futile,
　　When with troubles you're beset,
But remember you are facing
　　Just what other men have met.
You may fail, but fall still fighting;
　　Don't give up, whate'er you do;
Eyes front, head high to the finish.
　　See it through!

The Old, Old Story

I have no wish to rail at fate,
　　And vow that I'm unfairly treated;
I do not give vent to my hate
　　Because at times I am defeated.
Life has its ups and downs, I know,
　　But tell me why should people say
Whenever after fish I go:
　　"You should have been here yesterday"?

It is my luck always to strike
    A day when there is nothing doing,
When neither perch, nor bass, nor pike
    My baited hooks will come a-wooing.
Must I a day late always be?
    When not a nibble comes my way
Must someone always say to me:
    "We caught a bunch here yesterday"?

I am not prone to discontent,
    Nor over-zealous now to climb;
If victory is not yet meant
    For me I'll calmly bide my time.
But I should like just once to go
    Out fishing on some lake or bay
And not have someone mutter: "Oh,
    You should have been here yesterday."

The Pup

He tore the curtains yesterday,
    And scratched the paper on the wall;
Ma's rubbers, too, have gone astray—
    She says she left them in the hall;
He tugged the table cloth and broke
    A fancy saucer and a cup;
Though Bud and I think it a joke
    Ma scolds a lot about the pup.

The sofa pillows are a sight,
    The rugs are looking somewhat frayed,

And there is ruin, left and right,
    That little Boston bull has made.
He slept on Buddy's counterpane—
    Ma found him there when she woke up.
I think it needless to explain
    She scolds a lot about the pup.

And yet he comes and licks her hand
    And sometimes climbs into her lap
And there, Bud lets me understand,
    He very often takes his nap.
And Bud and I have learned to know
    She wouldn't give the rascal up:
She's really fond of him, although
    She scolds a lot about the pup.

The Little Hurts

Every night she runs to me
With a bandaged arm or a bandaged knee,
A stone-bruised heel or a swollen brow,
And in sorrowful tones she tells me how
She fell and "hurted herse'f to-day"
While she was having the "bestest play."

And I take her up in my arms and kiss
The new little wounds and whisper this:
"Oh, you must be careful, my little one,
You mustn't get hurt while your daddy's gone,
For every cut with its ache and smart
Leaves another bruise on your daddy's heart."

Every night I must stoop to see
The fresh little cuts on her arm or knee;
The little hurts that have marred her play,
And brought the tears on a happy day;
For the path of childhood is oft beset
With care and trouble and things that fret.

Oh, little girl, when you older grow,
Far greater hurts than these you'll know;
Greater bruises will bring your tears,
Around the bend of the lane of years,
But come to your daddy with them at night
And he'll do his best to make all things right.

The Stick-Together Families

The stick-together families are happier by far
Than the brothers and the sisters who take separate
    highways are.
The gladdest people living are the wholesome folks
    who make
A circle at the fireside that no power but death can
    break.
And the finest of conventions ever held beneath the
    sun
Are the little family gatherings when the busy day is
    done.

There are rich folk, there are poor folk, who imagine
    they are wise,

And they're very quick to shatter all the little family
 ties.
Each goes searching after pleasure in his own selected
 way,
Each with strangers likes to wander, and with
 strangers likes to play.
But it's bitterness they harvest, and it's empty joy
 they find,
For the children that are wisest are the stick-together
 kind.

There are some who seem to fancy that for gladness
 they must roam,
That for smiles that are the brightest they must
 wander far from home.
That the strange friend is the true friend, and they
 travel far astray
And they waste their lives in striving for a joy that's
 far away,
But the gladdest sort of people, when the busy day is
 done,
Are the brothers and the sisters who together share
 their fun.

It's the stick-together family that wins the joys of
 earth,
That hears the sweetest music and that finds the
 finest mirth;
It's the old home roof that shelters all the charm that
 life can give;

There you find the gladdest play-ground, there the
    happiest spot to live.
And, O weary, wandering brother, if contentment
    you would win,
Come you back unto the fireside and be comrade with
    your kin.

Grown-Up

Last year he wanted building blocks,
    And picture books and toys,
A saddle horse that gayly rocks,
    And games for little boys.
But now he's big and all that stuff
    His whim no longer suits;
He tells us that he's old enough
    To ask for rubber boots.

Last year whatever Santa brought
    Delighted him to own;
He never gave his wants a thought
    Nor made his wishes known.
But now he says he wants a gun,
    The kind that really shoots,
And I'm confronted with a son
    Demanding rubber boots.

The baby that we used to know
    Has somehow slipped away,

And when or where he chanced to go
    Not one of us can say.
But here's a helter-skelter lad
    That to me nightly scoots
And boldly wishes that he had
    A pair of rubber boots.

I'll bet old Santa Claus will sigh
    When down our flue he comes,
And seeks the babe that used to lie
    And suck his tiny thumbs,
And finds within that little bed
    A grown up boy who hoots
At building blocks, and wants instead
    A pair of rubber boots.

The Real Successes

You think that the failures are many,
    You think the successes are few,
But you judge by the rule of the penny,
    And not by the good that men do.
You judge men by standards of treasure
    That merely obtain upon earth,
When the brother you're snubbing may measure
    Full-length to God's standard of worth.

The failures are not in the ditches,
    The failures are not in the ranks,

They have missed the acquirement of riches,
    Their fortunes are not in the banks.
Their virtues are never paraded,
    Their worth is not always in view,
But they're fighting their battles unaided,
    And fighting them honestly, too.

There are failures to-day in high places
    The failures aren't all in the low;
There are rich men with scorn in their faces
    Whose homes are but castles of woe.
The homes that are happy are many,
    And numberless fathers are true;
And this is the standard, if any,
    By which we must judge what men do.

Wherever loved ones are awaiting
    The toiler to kiss and caress,
Though in Bradstreet's he hasn't a rating,
    He still is a splendid success.
If the dear ones who gather about him
    And know what he's striving to do
Have never a reason to doubt him,
    Is he less successful than you?

You think that the failures are many,
    You judge by men's profits in gold;
You judge by the rule of the penny—
    In this true success isn't told.

This falsely man's story is telling,
    For wealth often brings on distress,
But wherever love brightens a dwelling,
    There lives, rich or poor, a success.

The Sorry Hostess

She said she was sorry the weather was bad
The night that she asked us to dine;
And she really appeared inexpressibly sad
Because she had hoped 'twould be fine.
She was sorry to hear that my wife had a cold,
And she almost shed tears over that,
And how sorry she was, she most feelingly told,
That the steam wasn't on in the flat.

She was sorry she hadn't asked others to come,
She might just as well have had eight;
She said she was downcast and terribly glum
Because her dear husband was late.
She apologized then for the home she was in,
For the state of the rugs and the chairs,
For the children who made such a horrible din,
And then for the squeak in the stairs.

When the dinner began she apologized twice
For the olives, because they were small;
She was certain the celery, too, wasn't nice,
And the soup didn't suit her at all.

She was sorry she couldn't get whitefish instead
Of the trout that the fishmonger sent,
But she hoped that we'd manage somehow to be fed,
Though her dinner was not what she meant.

She spoke her regrets for the salad, and then
Explained she was really much hurt,
And begged both our pardons again and again
For serving a skimpy dessert.
She was sorry for this and sorry for that,
Though there really was nothing to blame.
But I thought to myself as I put on my hat,
Perhaps she is sorry we came.

The Little Old Man

The little old man with the curve in his back
And the eyes that are dim and the skin that is slack,
So slack that it wrinkles and rolls on his cheeks,
With a thin little voice that goes "crack!" when he
      speaks,
Never goes to the store but that right at his feet
Are all of the youngsters who live on the street.

And the little old man in the suit that was black,
And once might have perfectly fitted his back,
Has a boy's chubby fist in his own wrinkled hand,
And together they trudge off to Light-Hearted Land;
Some splendid excursions he gives every day
To the boys and the girls in his funny old way.

The little old man is as queer as can be;
He'd spend all his time with a child on his knee;
And the stories he tells I could never repeat,
But they're always of good boys and little girls sweet;
And the children come home at the end of the day
To tell what the little old man had to say.

Once the little old man didn't trudge to the store,
And the tap of his cane wasn't heard any more;
The children looked eagerly for him each day
And wondered why he didn't come out to play
Till some of them saw Doctor Brown ring his bell,
And they wept when they heard that he might not
      get well.

But after awhile he got out with his cane,
And called all the children around him again;
And I think as I see him go trudging along
In the center, once more, of his light-hearted throng,
That earth has no glory that's greater than this:
The little old man whom the children would miss.

The First Steps

Last night I held my arms to you
And you held yours to mine
And started out to march to me
As any soldier fine.
You lifted up your little feet
And laughingly advanced;

And I stood there and gazed upon
Your first wee steps, entranced.

You gooed and gurgled as you came
Without a sign of fear;
As though you knew, your journey o'er,
I'd greet you with a cheer.
And, what is more, you seemed to know,
Although you are so small,
That I was there, with eager arms,
To save you from a fall.

Three tiny steps you took, and then,
Disaster and dismay!
Your over-confidence had led
Your little feet astray.
You did not see what we could see
Nor fear what us alarms;
You stumbled, but ere you could fall
I caught you in my arms.

You little tyke, in days to come
You'll bravely walk alone,
And you may have to wander paths
Where dangers lurk unknown.
And, Oh, I pray that then, as now,
When accidents befall
You'll still remember that I'm near
To save you from a fall.

Signs

It's "be a good boy, Willie,"
  And it's "run away and play,
For Santa Claus is coming
  With his reindeer and his sleigh."
It's "mind what mother tells you,"
  And it's "put away your toys,
For Santa Claus is coming
  To the good girls and the boys."
Ho, Santa Claus is coming, there is Christmas in
    the air,
And little girls and little boys are good now every-
    where.

World-wide the little fellows
  Now are sweetly saying "please,"
And "thank you," and "excuse me,"
  And those little pleasantries
That good children are supposed to
  When there's company to hear;
And it's just as plain as can be
  That the Christmas time is near.
Ho, it's just as plain as can be that old Santa's on
    his way,
For there are no little children that are really bad
    to-day.

And when evening shadows lengthen,
  Every little curly head
Now is ready, aye, and willing
  To be tucked away in bed;

Not one begs to stay up longer,
  Not one even sheds a tear;
Ho, the goodness of the children
  Is a sign that Santa's near.
It's wonderful, the goodness of the little tots to-day,
When they know that good old Santa has begun to
        pack his sleigh.

When Mother Cooked with Wood

I do not quarrel with the gas,
  Our modern range is fine,
The ancient stove was doomed to pass
  From Time's grim firing line,
Yet now and then there comes to me
  The thought of dinners good
And pies and cake that used to be
  When mother cooked with wood.

The axe has vanished from the yard,
  The chopping block is gone,
There is no pile of cordwood hard
  For boys to work upon;
There is no box that must be filled
  Each morning to the hood;
Time in its ruthlessness has willed
  The passing of the wood.

And yet those days were fragrant days
  And spicy days and rare;

The kitchen knew a cheerful blaze
 And friendliness was there.
And every appetite was keen
 For breakfasts that were good
When I had scarcely turned thirteen
 And mother cooked with wood.

I used to dread my daily chore,
 I used to think it tough
When mother at the kitchen door
 Said I'd not chopped enough.
And on her baking days, I know,
 I shirked whene'er I could
In that now happy long ago
 When mother cooked with wood.

I never thought I'd wish to see
 That pile of wood again;
Back then it only seemed to me
 A source of care and pain.
But now I'd gladly give my all
 To stand where once I stood,
If those rare days I could recall
 When mother cooked with wood.

The Home Builders

The world is filled with bustle and with selfishness
 and greed,
It is filled with restless people that are dreaming of
 a deed.

You can read it in their faces; they are dreaming of
       the day
When they'll come to fame and fortune and put all
       their cares away.
And I think as I behold them, though it's far indeed
       they roam,
They will never find contentment save they seek for
       it at home.

I watch them as they hurry through the surging lines
       of men,
Spurred to speed by grim ambition, and I know
       they're dreaming then.
They are weary, sick and footsore, but their goal
       seems far away,
And it's little they've accomplished at the ending of
       the day.
It is rest they're vainly seeking, love and laughter
       in the gloam,
But they'll never come to claim it, save they claim it
       here at home.

For the peace that is the sweetest isn't born of minted
       gold,
And the joy that lasts the longest and still lingers
       when we're old
Is no dim and distant pleasure—it is not to-morrow's
       prize,
It is not the end of toiling, or the rainbow of our
       sighs.

It is every day within us—all the rest is hippo-
    drome—
And the soul that is the gladdest is the soul that
    builds a home.

They are fools who build for glory! They are fools
    who pin their hopes
On the come and go of battles or some vessel's
    slender ropes.
They shall sicken and shall wither and shall never
    peace attain
Who believe that real contentment only men vic-
    torious gain.
For the only happy toilers under earth's majestic
    dome
Are the ones who find their glories in the little spot
    called home.

Friends

Ain't it fine when things are going
    Topsy-turvy and askew
To discover someone showing
    Good old-fashioned faith in you?

Ain't it good when life seems dreary
    And your hopes about to end,
Just to feel the handclasp cheery
    Of a fine old loyal friend?

Gosh! one fellow to another
　　Means a lot from day to day,
Seems we're living for each other
　　In a friendly sort of way.

When a smile or cheerful greetin'
　　Means so much to fellows sore,
Seems we ought to keep repeatin'
　　Smiles an' praises more an' more.

October

Days are gettin' shorter an' the air a keener snap;
Apples now are droppin' into Mother Nature's lap;
The mist at dusk is risin' over valley, marsh an' fen
An' it's just as plain as sunshine, winter's comin' on
　　again.

The turkeys now are struttin' round the old farm-
　　house once more;
They are done with all their nestin', and their
　　hatchin' days are o'er;
Now the farmer's cuttin' fodder for the silo towerin'
　　high
An' he's frettin' an' complainin' 'cause the corn's a
　　bit too dry.

But the air is mighty peaceful an' the scene is good
　　to see,
An' there's somethin' in October that stirs deep in-
　　side o' me;

An' I just can't help believin' in a God above us when
Everything is ripe for harvest an' the frost is back
    again.

The Other Fellow

Whose luck is better far than ours?
                The other fellow's.
Whose road seems always lined with flowers?
                The other fellow's.
Who is the man who seems to get
Most joy in life, with least regret,
Who always seems to win his bet?
                The other fellow.

Who fills the place we think we'd like?
                The other fellow.
Whom does good fortune always strike?
                The other fellow.
Whom do we envy, day by day?
Who has more time than we to play?
Who is it, when we mourn, seems gay?
                The other fellow.

Who seems to miss the thorns we find?
                The other fellow.
Who seems to leave us all behind?
                The other fellow.
Who never seems to feel the woe,

The anguish and the pain we know?
Who gets the best seats at the show?
          The other fellow.

And yet, my friend, who envies you?
          The other fellow.
Who thinks he gathers only rue?
          The other fellow.
Who sighs because he thinks that he
Would infinitely happier be,
If he could be like you or me?
          The other fellow.

Send Her a Valentine

Send her a valentine to say
You love her in the same old way.
Just drop the long familiar ways
And live again the old-time days
When love was new and youth was bright
And all was laughter and delight,
And treat her as you would if she
Were still the girl that used to be.

Pretend that all the years have passed
Without one cold and wintry blast;
That you are coming still to woo
Your sweetheart as you used to do;
Forget that you have walked along
The paths of life where right and wrong

And joy and grief in battle are,
And play the heart without a scar.

Be what you were when youth was fine
And send to her a valentine;
Forget the burdens and the woe
That have been given you to know
And to the wife, so fond and true,
The pledges of the past renew.
'Twill cure her life of every ill
To find that you're her sweetheart still.

There Are No Gods

There are no gods that bring to youth
    The rich rewards that stalwarts claim;
The god of fortune is in truth
    A vision and an empty name.
The toiler who through doubt and care
    Unto his goal and victory plods,
With no one need his glory share:
    He is himself his favoring gods.

There are no gods that will bestow
    Earth's joys and blessings on a man.
Each one must choose the path he'll go,
    Then win from it what joy he can.
And he that battles with the odds
    Shall know success, but he who waits

The favors of the mystic gods,
   Shall never come to glory's gates.

No man is greater than his will;
   No gods to him will lend a hand!
Upon his courage and his skill
   The record of his life must stand.
What honors shall befall to him,
   What he shall claim of fame or pelf,
Depend not on the favoring whim
   Of fortune's god, but on himself.

The Little Church

The little church of Long Ago, where as a boy I sat
With mother in the family pew, and fumbled with
      my hat—
How I would like to see it now the way I saw it then,
The straight-backed pews, the pulpit high, the women
      and the men
Dressed stiffly in their Sunday clothes and solemnly
      devout,
Who closed their eyes when prayers were said and
      never looked about—
That little church of Long Ago, it wasn't grand to
      see,
But even as a little boy it meant a lot to me.

The choir loft where father sang comes back to me
      again;

I hear his tenor voice once more the way I heard it
      when
The deacons used to pass the plate, and once again I
      see
The people fumbling for their coins, as glad as they
      could be
To drop their quarters on the plate, and I'm a boy
      once more
With my two pennies in my fist that mother gave
      before
We left the house, and once again I'm reaching out to
      try
To drop them on the plate before the deacon passes
      by.

It seems to me I'm sitting in that high-backed pew,
      the while
The minister is preaching in that good old-fashioned
      style;
And though I couldn't understand it all somehow I
      know
The Bible was the text book in that church of Long
      Ago;
He didn't preach on politics, but used the word of
      God,
And even now I seem to see the people gravely nod,
As though agreeing thoroughly with all he had to
      say,
And then I see them thanking him before they go
      away.

The little church of Long Ago was not a structure
        huge,
It had no hired singers or no other subterfuge
To get the people to attend, 'twas just a simple place
Where every Sunday we were told about God's sav-
        ing grace;
No men of wealth were gathered there to help it with
        a gift;
The only worldly thing it had—a mortgage hard to
        lift.
And somehow, dreaming here to-day, I wish that I
        could know
The joy of once more sitting in that church of Long
        Ago.

The Old-Fashioned Thanksgiving

It may be I am getting old and like too much to dwell
Upon the days of bygone years, the days I loved so
        well;
But thinking of them now I wish somehow that I
        could know
A simple old Thanksgiving Day, like those of long
        ago,
When all the family gathered round a table richly
        spread,
With little Jamie at the foot and grandpa at the head,
The youngest of us all to greet the oldest with a smile,
With mother running in and out and laughing all the
        while.

It may be I'm old-fashioned, but it seems to me to-
day
We're too much bent on having fun to take the time
to pray;
Each little family grows up with fashions of its own;
It lives within a world itself and wants to be alone.
It has its special pleasures, its circle, too, of friends;
There are no get-together days; each one his journey
wends,
Pursuing what he likes the best in his particular way,
Letting the others do the same upon Thanksgiving
Day.

I like the olden way the best, when relatives were
glad
To meet the way they used to do when I was but a
lad;
The old home was a rendezvous for all our kith and
kin,
And whether living far or near they all came trooping
in
With shouts of "Hello, daddy!" as they fairly
stormed the place
And made a rush for mother, who would stop to wipe
her face
Upon her gingham apron before she kissed them all,
Hugging them proudly to her breast, the grownups
and the small.

Then laughter rang throughout the home, and, Oh,
the jokes they told;

From Boston, Frank brought new ones, but father
     sprang the old;
All afternoon we chatted, telling what we hoped to
     do,
The struggles we were making and the hardships
     we'd gone through;
We gathered round the fireside. How fast the hours
     would fly—
It seemed before we'd settled down 'twas time to say
     good-bye.
Those were the glad Thanksgivings, the old-time
     families knew
When relatives could still be friends and every heart
     was true.

The Broken Drum

There is sorrow in the household;
There's a grief too hard to bear;
There's a little cheek that's tear-stained;
There's a sobbing baby there.
And try how we will to comfort,
Still the tiny teardrops come;
For, to solve a vexing problem,
Curly Locks has wrecked his drum.

It had puzzled him and worried,
How the drum created sound;
For he couldn't understand it;
It was not enough to pound

With his tiny hands and drumsticks,
And at last the day has come,
When another hope is shattered;
Now in ruins lies his drum.

With his metal bank he broke it,
Tore the tightened skin aside,
Gazed on vacant space bewildered,
Then he broke right down and cried.
For the broken bubble shocked him
And the baby tears must come;
Now a joy has gone forever:
Curly Locks has wrecked his drum.

While his mother tries to soothe him,
I am sitting here alone;
In the life that lies behind me,
Many shocks like that I've known.
And the boy who's upstairs weeping,
In the years that are to come
Will learn that many pleasures
Are as empty as his drum.

As It Is

I might wish the world were better,
    I might sit around and sigh
For a water that is wetter
    And a bluer sort of sky.

There are times I think the weather
    Could be much improved upon,
But when taken altogether
    It's a good old world we're on.
I might tell how I would make it,
    But when I have had my say
It is still my job to take it
    As it is, from day to day.

I might wish that men were kinder,
    And less eager after gold;
I might wish that they were blinder
    To the faults they now behold.
And I'd try to make them gentle,
    And more tolerant in strife
And a bit more sentimental
    O'er the finer things of life.
But I am not here to make them,
    Or to work in human clay;
It is just my work to take them
    As they are from day to day.

Here's a world that suffers sorrow,
    Here are bitterness and pain,
And the joy we plan to-morrow
    May be ruined by the rain.
Here are hate and greed and badness,
    Here are love and friendship, too,
But the most of it is gladness
    When at last we've run it through.

Could we only understand it
   As we shall some distant day,
We should see that He who planned it
   Knew our needs along the way.

America

God has been good to men. He gave
His Only Son their souls to save,
And then he made a second gift,
Which from their dreary lives should lift
The tyrant's yoke and set them free
From all who'd throttle liberty.
He gave America to men—
Fashioned this land we love, and then
Deep in her forest sowed the seed
Which was to serve man's earthly need.

When wisps of smoke first upwards curled
From pilgrim fires, upon the world
Unnoticed and unseen, began
God's second work of grace for man.
Here where the savage roamed and fought,
God sowed the seed of nobler thought;
Here to the land we love to claim,
The pioneers of freedom came;
Here has been cradled all that's best
In every human mind and breast.

For full four hundred years and more
Our land has stretched her welcoming shore

To weary feet from soils afar;
Soul-shackled serfs of king and czar
Have journeyed here and toiled and sung
And talked of freedom to their young,
And God above has smiled to see
This precious work of liberty,
And watched this second gift He gave
The dreary lives of men to save.

And now, when liberty's at bay,
And blood-stained tyrants force the fray,
Worn warriors, battling for the right,
Crushed by oppression's cruel might,
Hear in the dark through which they grope
America's glad cry of hope:
Man's liberty is not to die!
America is standing by!
World-wide shall human lives be free:
America has crossed the sea!

America! the land we love!
God's second gift from Heaven above,
Builded and fashioned out of truth,
Sinewed by Him with splendid youth
For that glad day when shall be furled
All tyrant flags throughout the world.
For this our banner holds the sky:
That liberty shall never die.
For this, America began:
To make a brotherhood of man.

Memorial Day

The finest tribute we can pay
Unto our hero dead to-day,
Is not a rose wreath, white and red,
In memory of the blood they shed;
It is to stand beside each mound,
Each couch of consecrated ground,
And pledge ourselves as warriors true
Unto the work they died to do.

Into God's valleys where they lie
At rest, beneath the open sky,
Triumphant now, o'er every foe,
As living tributes let us go.
No wreath of rose or immortelles
Or spoken word or tolling bells
Will do to-day, unless we give
Our pledge that liberty shall live.

Our hearts must be the roses red
We place above our hero dead;
To-day beside their graves we must
Renew allegiance to their trust;
Must bare our heads and humbly say
We hold the Flag as dear as they,
And stand, as once they stood, to die
To keep the Stars and Stripes on high.

The finest tribute we can pay
Unto our hero dead to-day

Is not of speech or roses red,
But living, throbbing hearts instead
That shall renew the pledge they sealed
With death upon the battlefield:
That freedom's flag shall bear no stain
And free men wear no tyrant's chain.

Spoiling Them

"You're spoiling them!" the mother cries
When I give way to weepy eyes
And let them do the things they wish,
Like cleaning up the jelly dish,
Or finishing the chocolate cake,
Or maybe let the rascal take
My piece of huckleberry pie,
Because he wants it more than I.

"You're spoiling them!" the mother tells,
When I am heedless to their yells,
And let them race and romp about
And do not put their joy to rout.
I know I should be firm, and yet
I tried it once to my regret;
I will remember till I'm old
The day I started in to scold.

I stamped my foot and shouted: "Stop!"
And Bud just let his drum sticks drop,
And looked at me, and turned away;
That night there was no further play.

The girls were solemn-like and still,
Just as girls are when they are ill,
And when unto his cot I crept,
I found him sobbing as he slept.

That was my first attempt and last
To play the scold. I'm glad it passed
So quickly and has left no trace
Of memory on each little face;
But now when mother whispers low:
"You're spoiling them," I answer, "No!
But it is plain, as plain can be,
Those little tykes are spoiling me."

Faces

I look into the faces of the people passing by,
    The glad ones and the sad ones, and the lined with
        misery,
And I wonder why the sorrow or the twinkle in the
    eye;
    But the pale and weary faces are the ones that
        trouble me.

I saw a face this morning, and time was when it was
    fair;
    Youth had brushed it bright with color in the
        distant long ago,
And the goddess of the lovely once had kept a temple
    there,

But the cheeks were pale with grieving and the
    eyes were dull with woe.

Who has done this thing I wondered; what has
    wrought the ruin here?
  Why these sunken cheeks and pallid where the
    roses once were pink?
Why has beauty fled her palace; did some vandal
    hand appear?
  Did her lover prove unfaithful or her husband
    take to drink?

Once the golden voice of promise whispered sweetly
    in her ears;
  She was born to be a garden where the smiles of
    love might lurk;
Now the eyes that shone like jewels are but gateways
    for her tears,
  And she takes her place among us, toilers early
    bound for work.

Is it fate that writes so sadly, or the cruelty of man?
  What foul deed has marred the parchment of a life
    so fair as this?
Who has wrecked this lovely temple and destroyed
    the Maker's plan,
  Raining blows on cheeks of beauty God had fash-
    ioned just to kiss?

Oh, the pale and weary faces of the people that I see
  Are the ones that seem to haunt me, and I pray to
    God above

That such cruel desolation shall not ever come to be
   Stamped forever in the future on the faces that I
   love.

The Doctor

I don't see why Pa likes him so,
   And seems so glad to have him come;
He jabs my ribs and wants to know
   If here and there it's hurting some.
He holds my wrist, coz there are things
   In there, which always jump and jerk,
Then, with a telephone he brings,
   He listens to my breather work.

He taps my back and pinches me,
   Then hangs a mirror on his head
And looks into my throat to see
   What makes it hurt and if it's red.
Then on his knee he starts to write
   And says to mother, with a smile:
"This ought to fix him up all right,
   We'll cure him in a little while."

I don't see why Pa likes him so.
   Whenever I don't want to play
He says: "The boy is sick, I know!
   Let's get the doctor right away."
And when he comes, he shakes his hand,
   And hustles him upstairs to me,

And seems contented just to stand
　　Inside the room where he can see.

Then Pa says every time he goes:
　　"That's money I am glad to pay;
It's worth it, when a fellow knows
　　His pal will soon be up to play."
But maybe if my Pa were me,
　　And had to take his pills and all,
He wouldn't be so glad to see
　　The doctor come to make a call.

Compensation

I'd like to think when life is done
　　That I had filled a needed post,
That here and there I'd paid my fare
　　With more than idle talk and boast;
That I had taken gifts divine,
The breath of life and manhood fine,
And tried to use them now and then
In service for my fellow men.

I'd hate to think when life is through
　　That I had lived my round of years
A useless kind, that leaves behind
　　No record in this vale of tears;
That I had wasted all my days
By treading only selfish ways,
And that this world would be the same
If it had never known my name.

I'd like to think that here and there,
    When I am gone, there shall remain
A happier spot that might have not
    Existed had I toiled for gain;
That some one's cheery voice and smile
Shall prove that I had been worth while;
That I had paid with something fine
My debt to God for life divine.

It Couldn't Be Done

Somebody said that it couldn't be done,
    But he with a chuckle replied
That "maybe it couldn't," but he would be one
    Who wouldn't say so till he'd tried.
So he buckled right in with the trace of a grin
    On his face. If he worried he hid it.
He started to sing as he tackled the thing
    That couldn't be done, and he did it.

Somebody scoffed: "Oh, you'll never do that;
    At least no one ever has done it";
But he took off his coat and he took off his hat,
    And the first thing we knew he'd begun it.
With a lift of his chin and a bit of a grin,
    Without any doubting or quiddit,
He started to sing as he tackled the thing
    That couldn't be done, and he did it.

There are thousands to tell you it cannot be done,
    There are thousands to prophesy failure;

There are thousands to point out to you one by one,
    The dangers that wait to assail you.
But just buckle in with a bit of a grin,
    Just take off your coat and go to it;
Just start in to sing as you tackle the thing
    That "cannot be done," and you'll do it.

The Furnace Door

My father is a peaceful man;
He tries in every way he can
To live a life of gentleness
And patience all the while.
He says that needless fretting's vain,
That it's absurd to be profane,
That nearly every wrong can be
Adjusted with a smile.
Yet try no matter how he will,
There's one thing that annoys him still,
One thing that robs him of his calm
And leaves him very sore;
He cannot keep his self-control
When with a shovel full of coal
He misses where it's headed for,
And hits the furnace door.

He measures with a careful eye
The space for which he's soon to try,
Then grabs his trusty shovel up
And loads it in the bin,

Then turns and with a healthy lunge,
That's two parts swing and two parts plunge,
He lets go at the furnace fire,
Convinced it will go in!
And then we hear a sudden smack,
The cellar air turns blue and black;
Above the rattle of the coal
We hear his awful roar.
From dreadful language upward hissed
We know that father's aim has missed,
And that his shovel full of coal
Went up against the door.

The minister was here one day
For supper, and Pa went away
To fix the furnace fire, and soon
We heard that awful roar.
And through the furnace pipes there came
Hot words that made Ma blush for shame.
"It strikes me," said the minister,
"He hit the furnace door."
Ma turned away and hung her head;
"I'm so ashamed," was all she said.
And then the minister replied:
"Don't worry. I admit
That when I hit the furnace door,
And spill the coal upon the floor,
I quite forget the cloth I wear
And—er—swear a little bit."

Out Fishin'

A feller isn't thinkin' mean,
    Out fishin';
His thoughts are mostly good an' clean,
    Out fishin'.
He doesn't knock his fellow men,
Or harbor any grudges then;
A feller's at his finest when
    Out fishin'.

The rich are comrades to the poor,
    Out fishin';
All brothers of a common lure,
    Out fishin'.
The urchin with the pin an' string
Can chum with millionaire an' king;
Vain pride is a forgotten thing,
    Out fishin'.

A feller gits a chance to dream,
    Out fishin';
He learns the beauties of a stream,
    Out fishin';
An' he can wash his soul in air
That isn't foul with selfish care,
An' relish plain and simple fare,
    Out fishin'.

A feller has no time fer hate,
    Out fishin';

He isn't eager to be great,
    Out fishin'.
He isn't thinkin' thoughts of pelf,
Or goods stacked high upon a shelf,
But he is always just himself,
    Out fishin'.

A feller's glad to be a friend,
    Out fishin';
A helpin' hand he'll always lend,
    Out fishin'.
The brotherhood of rod an' line
An' sky and stream is always fine;
Men come real close to God's design,
    Out fishin'.

A feller isn't plotting schemes,
    Out fishin';
He's only busy with his dreams,
    Out fishin'.
His livery is a coat of tan,
His creed—to do the best he can;
A feller's always mostly man,
    Out fishin'.

Tied Down

"They tie you down," a woman said,
Whose cheeks should have been flaming red

With shame to speak of children so.
"When babies come you cannot go
In search of pleasure with your friends,
And all your happy wandering ends.
The things you like you cannot do,
For babies make a slave of you."

I looked at her and said: " 'Tis true
That children make a slave of you,
And tie you down with many a knot,
But have you never thought to what
It is of happiness and pride
That little babies have you tied?
Do you not miss the greater joys
That come with little girls and boys?

"They tie you down to laughter rare,
To hours of smiles and hours of care,
To nights of watching and to fears;
Sometimes they tie you down to tears
And then repay you with a smile,
And make your trouble all worth while.
They tie you fast to chubby feet,
And cheeks of pink and kisses sweet.

"They fasten you with cords of love
To God divine, who reigns above.
They tie you, whereso'er you roam,
Unto the little place called home;
And over sea or railroad track
They tug at you to bring you back.

The happiest people in the town
Are those the babies have tied down.

"Oh, go your selfish way and free,
But hampered I would rather be,
Yes rather than a kingly crown
I would be, what you term, tied down;
Tied down to dancing eyes and charms,
Held fast by chubby, dimpled arms,
The fettered slave of girl and boy,
And win from them earth's finest joy."

Aunty

I'm sorry for a feller if he hasn't any aunt,
To let him eat and do the things his mother says he
    can't.
An aunt to come a visitin' or one to go and see
Is just about the finest kind of lady there could be.
Of course she's not your mother, an' she hasn't got
    her ways,
But a part that's most important in a feller's life she
    plays.

She is kind an' she is gentle, an' sometimes she's full
    of fun,
An' she's very sympathetic when some dreadful thing
    you've done.
An' she likes to buy you candy, an' she's always
    gettin' toys

That you wish your Pa would get you, for she hasn't
      any boys.
But sometimes she's over-loving, an' your cheeks turn
      red with shame
When she smothers you with kisses, but you like her
      just the same.

One time my father took me to my aunty's, an' he
      said:
"You will stay here till I get you, an' be sure you go
      to bed
When your aunty says it's time to, an' be good an'
      mind her, too,
An' when you come home we'll try to have a big
      surprise for you."
I did as I was told to, an' when Pa came back for me
He said there was a baby at the house for me to see.

I've been visitin' at aunty's for a week or two, an'
      Pa
Has written that he's comin' soon to take me home
      to Ma.
He says they're gettin' lonely, an' I'm kind o' lonely,
      too,
Coz an aunt is not exactly what your mother is to
      you.
I am hungry now to see her, but I'm wondering to-
      day
If Pa's bought another baby in the time I've been
      away.

Toys and Life

You can learn a lot from boys
By the way they use their toys;
Some are selfish in their care,
Never very glad to share
Playthings with another boy;
Seem to want to hoard their joy.
And they hide away the drum
For the days that never come;
Hide the train of cars and skates,
Keeping them from all their mates,
And run all their boyhood through
With their toys as good as new.

Others gladly give and lend,
Heedless that the tin may bend,
Caring not that drum-heads break,
Minding not that playmates take
To themselves the joy that lies
In the little birthday prize.
And in homes that house such boys
Always there are broken toys,
Symbolizing moments glad
That the youthful lives have had.
There you'll never find a shelf
Dedicated unto self.

Toys are made for children's fun,
Very frail and quickly done,

And who keeps them long to view,
Bright of paint and good as new,
Robs himself and other boys
Of their swiftly passing joys.
So he looked upon a toy
When our soldier was a boy;
And somehow to-day we're glad
That the tokens of our lad
And the trinkets that we keep
Are a broken, battered heap.

Life itself is but a toy
Filled with duty and with joy;
Not too closely should we guard
Our brief time from being scarred;
Never high on musty shelves
Should we hoard it for ourselves.
It is something we should share
In another's hour of care—
Something we should gladly give
That another here may live;
We should never live it through
Keeping it as good as new.

The Burden Bearer

Oh, my shoulders grow aweary of the burdens I am
    bearin',
An' I grumble when I'm footsore at the rough road
    I am farin',

But I strap my knapsack tighter till I feel the leather
     bind me,
An' I'm glad to bear the burdens for the ones who
     come behind me.
It's for them that I am ploddin', for the children
     comin' after;
I would strew their path with roses and would fill
     their days with laughter.

Oh, there's selfishness within me, there are times it
     gets to talkin',
Times I hear it whisper to me, "It's a dusty road
     you're walkin';
Why not rest your feet a little; why not pause an'
     take your leisure?
Don't you hunger in your strivin' for the merry whirl
     of pleasure?"
Then I turn an' see them smilin' an' I grip my burdens
     tighter,
For the joy that I am seekin' is to see their eyes grow
     brighter.

Oh, I've sipped the cup of sorrow an' I've felt the
     gad of trouble,
An' I know the hurt of trudgin' through a field
     o'errun with stubble;
But a rougher road to travel had my father good
     before me,
An' I'm owin' all my gladness to the tasks he shoul-
     dered for me.

Oh, I didn't understand it, when a lad I played about
    him,
But he labored for my safety in the days I'd be with-
    out him.

Oh, my kindly father never gave himself a year of
    leisure—
Never lived one selfish moment, never turned aside
    for pleasure—
Though he must have grown aweary of the burdens
    he was bearin';
He was tryin' hard to better every road I'd soon be
    farin'.
Now I turn an' see them smilin' an' I hear their merry
    laughter,
An' I'm glad to bear the burdens for the ones that
    follow after.

Good Business

If I possessed a shop or store,
I'd drive the grouches off my floor;
I'd never let some gloomy guy
Offend the folks who came to buy;
I'd never keep a boy or clerk
With mental toothache at his work,
Nor let a man who draws my pay
Drive customers of mine away.

I'd treat the man who takes my time
And spends a nickel or a dime

With courtesy and make him feel
That I was pleased to close the deal,
Because tomorrow, who can tell?
He may want stuff I have to sell,
And in that case then glad he'll be
To spend his dollars all with me.

The reason people pass one door
To patronize another store,
Is not because the busier place
Has better silks or gloves or lace,
Or cheaper prices, but it lies
In pleasant words and smiling eyes;
The only difference, I believe,
Is in the treatment folks receive.

It is good business to be fair,
To keep a bright and cheerful air
About the place, and not to show
Your customers how much you know;
Whatever any patron did
I'd try to keep my temper hid,
And never let him spread along
The word that I had done him wrong.

"It's a Boy"

The doctor leads a busy life, he wages war with
    death;
Long hours he spends to help the one who's fighting
    hard for breath;

He cannot call his time his own, nor share in others'
       fun,
His duties claim him through the night when others'
       work is done.
And yet the doctor seems to be God's messenger of
       joy,
Appointed to announce this news of gladness: "It's
       a boy!"

In many ways unpleasant is the doctor's round of
       cares,
I should not like to have to bear the burdens that he
       bears;
His eyes must look on horrors grim, unmoved he
       must remain,
Emotion he must master if he hopes to conquer pain;
Yet to his lot this duty falls, his voice he must employ
To speak to man the happiest phrase that's sounded:
       "It's a boy!"

I wish 'twere given me to speak a message half so
       glad
As that the doctor brings unto the fear-distracted dad.
I wish that simple words of mine could change the
       skies to blue,
And lift the care from troubled hearts, as those he
       utters do.
I wish that I could banish all the thoughts that man
       annoy,
And cheer him as the doctor does, who whispers:
       "It's a boy."

Whoever through the hours of night has stood outside her door,
And wondered if she'd smile again; whoe'er has paced the floor,
And lived those years of fearful thoughts, and then been swept from woe
Up to the topmost height of bliss that's given man to know,
Will tell you there's no phrase so sweet, so charged with human joy
As that the doctor brings from God—that message: "It's a boy!"

Becoming a Dad

Old women say that men don't know
The pain through which all mothers go,
And maybe that is true, and yet
I vow I never shall forget
The night he came.   I suffered, too,
Those bleak and dreary long hours through:
I paced the floor and mopped my brow
And waited for his glad wee-ow!
I went upstairs and then came down,
Because I saw the doctor frown
And knew beyond the slightest doubt
He wished to goodness I'd clear out.

I walked into the yard for air
And back again to hear her there,

And met the nurse, as calm as though
My world was not in deepest woe,
And when I questioned, seeking speech
Of consolation that would reach
Into my soul and strengthen me
For dreary hours that were to be:
"Progressing nicely!" that was all
She said and tip-toed down the hall;
"Progressing nicely!" nothing more,
And left me there to pace the floor.

And once the nurse came out in haste
For something that had been misplaced,
And I that had been growing bold
Then felt my blood grow icy cold;
And fear's stern chill swept over me.
I stood and watched and tried to see
Just what it was she came to get.
I haven't learned that secret yet.
I half-believe that nurse in white
Was adding fuel to my fright
And taking an unholy glee,
From time to time, in torturing me.

Then silence! To her room I crept
And was informed the doctor slept!
The doctor slept! Oh, vicious thought,
While she at death's door bravely fought
And suffered untold anguish deep,
The doctor lulled himself to sleep.

I looked and saw him stretched out flat
And could have killed the man for that.
Then morning broke, and oh, the joy;
With dawn there came to us our boy,
And in a glorious little while
I went in there and saw her smile!

I must have looked a human wreck,
My collar wilted at the neck,
My hair awry, my features drawn
With all the suffering I had borne.
She looked at me and softly said,
"If I were you, I'd go to bed."
Hers was the bitterer part, I know;
She traveled through the vale of woe,
But now when women folks recall
The pain and anguish of it all
I answer them in manner sad:
"It's no cinch to become a dad."

The Simple Things

I would not be too wise—so very wise
  That I must sneer at simple songs and creeds,
And let the glare of wisdom blind my eyes
  To humble people and their humble needs.

I would not care to climb so high that I
  Could never hear the children at their play,
Could only see the people passing by,
  And never hear the cheering words they say.

I would not know too much—too much to smile
    At trivial errors of the heart and hand,
Nor be too proud to play the friend the while,
    Nor cease to help and know and understand.

I would not care to sit upon a throne,
    Or build my house upon a mountain-top,
Where I must dwell in glory all alone
    And never friend come in or poor man stop.

God grant that I may live upon this earth
    And face the tasks which every morning brings
And never lose the glory and the worth
    Of humble service and the simple things.

When the Minister Calls

My Paw says that it used to be,
Whenever the minister came for tea,
'At they sat up straight in their chairs at night
An' put all their common things out o' sight,
An' nobody cracked a joke or grinned,
But they talked o' the way that people sinned,
An' the burnin' fires that would cook you sure
When you came to die, if you wasn't pure—
Such a gloomy affair it used to be
Whenever the minister came for tea.

But now when the minister comes to call
I get him out for a game of ball,

And you'd never know if you'd see him bat,
Without any coat or vest or hat,
That he is a minister, no, siree!
He looks like a regular man to me.
An' he knows just how to go down to the dirt
For the grounders hot without gettin' hurt—
An' when they call us, both him an' me
Have to git washed up again for tea.

Our minister says if you'll just play fair
You'll be fit for heaven or anywhere;
An' fun's all right if your hands are clean
An' you never cheat an' you don't get mean.
He says that he never has understood
Why a feller can't play an' still be good.
An' my Paw says that he's just the kind
Of a minister that he likes to find—
So I'm always tickled as I can be
Whenever our minister comes for tea.

Father to Son

The times have proved my judgment bad.
    I've followed foolish hopes in vain,
And as you look upon your dad
    You see him commonplace and plain.
No brilliant wisdom I enjoy;
    The jests I tell have grown to bore you,
But just remember this, my boy:
    'Twas I who chose your mother for you!

Against the blunders I have made
   And all the things I've failed to do,
The weaknesses which I've displayed,
   This fact remains forever true;
This to my credit still must stay
   And don't forget it, I implore you;
Whatever else you think or say:
   'Twas I who chose your mother for you!

Chuckle at times behind my back
   About the ties and hats I wear.
Sound judgment I am known to lack.
   Smile at the ancient views I air.
Say if you will I'm often wrong,
   But with my faults strewn out before you,
Remember this your whole life long:
   'Twas I who chose your mother for you!

Your life from babyhood to now
   Has known the sweetness of her care;
Her tender hand has soothed your brow;
   Her love gone with you everywhere.
Through every day and every night
   You've had an angel to adore you.
So bear in mind I once was right:
   'Twas I who chose your mother for you!

Nothing to Laugh At

'Tain't nothin' to laugh at as I can see!
If you'd been stung by a bumble bee,

An' your nose wuz swelled an' it smarted, too,
You wouldn't want people to laugh at you.
If you had a lump that wuz full of fire,
Like you'd been touched by a red hot wire,
An' your nose spread out like a load of hay,
You wouldn't want strangers who come your way
To ask you to let 'em see the place
An' laugh at you right before your face.

What's funny about it, I'd like to know?
It isn't a joke to be hurted so!
An' how wuz I ever on earth to tell
'At the pretty flower which I stooped to smell
In our backyard wuz the very one
Which a bee wuz busily working on?
An' jus' as I got my nose down there,
He lifted his foot an' kicked for fair,
An' he planted his stinger right into me,
But it's nothin' to laugh at as I can see.

I let out a yell an' my Maw came out
To see what the trouble wuz all about.
She says from my shriek she wuz sure 'at I
Had been struck by a motor car passin' by;
But when she found what the matter wuz
She laughed just like ever'body does
An' she made me stand while she poked about
To pull his turrible stinger out.
An' my Pa laughed, too, when he looked at me,
But it's nothin' to laugh at, as I can see.

My Maw put witch hazel on the spot
To take down the swellin' but it has not.
It seems to git bigger as time goes by
An' I can't see good out o' this one eye;
An' it hurts clean down to my very toes
Whenever I've got to blow my nose.
An' all I can say is when this gits well
There ain't any flowers I'll stoop to smell.
I'm through disturbin' a bumble bee,
But it's nothin' to laugh at, as I can see.

Little Girls Are Best

Little girls are mighty nice,
    Take 'em any way they come;
They are always worth their price;
    Life without 'em would be glum;
Run earth's lists of treasures through,
    Pile 'em high until they fall,
Gold an' costly jewels, too—
    Little girls are best of all.

Nothing equals 'em on earth!
    I'm an old man an' I know
Any little girl is worth
    More than all the gold below;
Eyes o' blue or brown or gray,
    Raven hair or golden curls,
There's no joy on earth to-day
    Quite so fine as little girls.

Pudgy nose or freckled face,
  Fairy-like or plain to see,
God has surely blessed the place
  Where a little girl may be;
They're the jewels of His crown
  Dropped to earth from heaven above,
Like wee angel souls sent down
  To remind us of His love.

God has made some lovely things—
  Roses red an' skies o' blue,
Trees an' babbling silver springs,
  Gardens glistening with dew—
But take every gift to man,
  Big an' little, great an' small,
Judge it on its merits, an'
  Little girls are best of all!

She Powders Her Nose

A woman is queer, there's no doubt about that.
She hates to be thin and she hates to be fat;
One minute it's laughter, the next it's a cry—
You can't understand her, however you try;
But there's one thing about her which everyone
  knows—
A woman's not dressed till she powders her nose.

You never can tell what a woman will say;
She's a law to herself every hour of the day.

It keeps a man guessing to know what to do,
And mostly he's wrong when his guessing is through;
But this you can bet on, wherever she goes
She'll find some occasion to powder her nose.

I've studied the sex for a number of years;
I've watched her in laughter and seen her in tears;
On her ways and her whims I have pondered a lot,
To find what will please her and just what will not;
But all that I've learned from the start to the close
Is that sooner or later she'll powder her nose.

At church or a ball game, a dance or a show,
There's one thing about her I know that I know—
At weddings or funerals, dinners of taste,
You can bet that her hand will dive into her waist,
And every few minutes she'll strike up a pose,
And the whole world must wait till she powders her
    nose.

All for the Best

Things mostly happen for the best.
However hard it seems to-day,
When some fond plan has gone astray
Or what you've wished for most is lost
An' you sit countin' up the cost
With eyes half-blind by tears o' grief
While doubt is chokin' out belief,
You'll find when all is understood
That what seemed bad was really good.

Life can't be counted in a day.
The present rain that will not stop
Next autumn means a bumper crop.
We wonder why some things must be—
Care's purpose we can seldom see—
An' yet long afterwards we turn
To view the past, an' then we learn
That what once filled our minds with doubt
Was good for us as it worked out.

I've never known an hour of care
But that I've later come to see
That it has brought some joy to me.
Even the sorrows I have borne,
Leavin' me lonely an' forlorn
An' hurt an' bruised an' sick at heart,
In life's great plan have had a part.
An' though I could not understand
Why I should bow to Death's command,
As time went on I came to know
That it was really better so.

Things mostly happen for the best.
So narrow is our vision here
That we are blinded by a tear
An' stunned by every hurt an' blow
Which comes to-day to strike us low.
An' yet some day we turn an' find
That what seemed cruel once was kind.
Most things, I hold, are wisely planned
If we could only understand.

With Dog and Gun

Out in the woods with a dog an' gun
Is my idee of a real day's fun.
'Tain't the birds that I'm out to kill
That furnish me with the finest thrill,
'Cause I never worry or fret a lot,
Or curse my luck if I miss a shot.
There's many a time, an' I don't know why,
That I shoot too low or I aim too high,
An' all I can see is the distant whirr
Of a bird that's gittin' back home to her—
Yep, gittin' back home at the end o' day,
An' I'm just as glad that he got away.

There's a whole lot more in the woods o' fall
Than the birds you bag—if you think at all.
There's colors o' gold an' red an' brown
As never were known in the busy town;
There's room to breathe in the purest air
An' something worth looking at everywhere;
There's the dog who's leadin' you on an' on
To a patch o' cover where birds have gone,
An' standin' there, without move or change,
Till you give the sign that you've got the range.
That's thrill enough for my blood, I say,
So why should I care if they get away?

Fact is, there are times that I'd ruther miss
Than to bring 'em down, 'cause I feel like this:

There's a heap more joy in a living thing
Than a breast crushed in or a broken wing,
An' I can't feel right, an' I never will,
When I look at a bird that I've dared to kill.
Oh, I'm jus' plumb happy to tramp about
An' follow my dog as he hunts 'em out,
Jus' watchin' him point in his silent way
Where the Bob Whites are an' the partridge stay;
For the joy o' the great outdoors I've had,
So why should I care if my aim is bad?

The Making of Friends

If nobody smiled and nobody cheered and nobody
    helped us along,
If each every minute looked after himself and good
    things all went to the strong,
If nobody cared just a little for you, and nobody
    thought about me,
And we stood all alone to the battle of life, what a
    dreary old world it would be!

If there were no such a thing as a flag in the sky as a
    symbol of comradeship here,
If we lived as the animals live in the woods, with
    nothing held sacred or dear,
And selfishness ruled us from birth to the end, and
    never a neighbor had we,
And never we gave to another in need, what a dreary
    old world it would be!

Oh, if we were rich as the richest on earth and strong
    as the strongest that lives,
Yet never we knew the delight and the charm of the
    smile which the other man gives,
If kindness were never a part of ourselves, though
    we owned all the land we could see,
And friendship meant nothing at all to us here, what
    a dreary old world it would be!

Life is sweet just because of the friends we have
    made and the things which in common we share;
We want to live on not because of ourselves, but
    because of the people who care;
It's giving and doing for somebody else—on that
    all life's splendor depends,
And the joy of this world, when you've summed it
    all up, is found in the making of friends.

Dirty Hands

I have to wash myself at night before I go to bed,
An' wash again when I get up, and wash before I'm
    fed,
An' Ma inspects my neck an' ears an' Pa my hands
    an' shirt—
They seem to wonder why it is that I'm so fond of
    dirt.
But Bill—my chum—an' I agree that we have never
    seen
A feller doing anything whose hands were white an'
    clean.

Bill's mother scolds the same as mine an' calls him
    in from play
To make him wash his face an' hands a dozen times
    a day.
Dirt seems to worry mothers so. But when the
    plumber comes
To fix the pipes, it's plain to see he never scrubs his
    thumbs;
His clothes are always thick with grease, his face is
    smeared with dirt,
An' he is not ashamed to show the smudges on his
    shirt.

The motorman who runs the car has hands much
    worse than mine,
An' I have noticed when we ride there's dirt in every
    line.
The carpenter who works around our house can mend
    a chair
Or put up shelves or fix the floor, an' mother doesn't
    care
That he's not in his Sunday best; she never interferes
An' makes him stop his work to go upstairs to wash
    his ears.

The fellers really doing things, as far as I can see,
Have hands and necks and ears that are as dirty as
    can be.
The man who fixes father's car when he can't make
    it go,
Most always has a smudgy face—his hands aren't
    white as snow.

But I must wash an' wash an' wash while everybody
    knows
The most important men in town have dirty hands
    and clo'es.

Football

I'd rather fancied it would come, a healthy boy who's
    ten years old
Forecasts the things he'll want to do without his
    secrets being told;
And so last night when I got home and found his
    mother strangely still,
I guessed somehow that mother love had battled with
    a youngster's will.
"You'll have to settle it," said she; "there's nothing
    more that I can say,
The game of football's calling him and he insists he
    wants to play."

We've talked it over many a time; we've hoped he
    wouldn't choose the game,
And I suppose there's not a boy whose parents do
    not feel the same.
They dread, as we, the rugged sport; they wonder,
    too, just what they'll say
When son of theirs comes home, as ours, and begs
    to be allowed to play.

And now the question's up to me, a question that
    I can't evade,
But football is a manly game and I am glad he's not
    afraid.

He wants to play, he says to me; he knows the game
    is rough and grim,
But worse than hurt and broken bones is what his
    friends will think of him;
"They'd call me yellow," he explained, "if I stay out."
    Of all things here
There's nothing quite so hard to bear as is the heart-
    less gibe or jeer,
And though I cannot spare him pain or hurt when
    tackles knock him flat,
Being his father, I've said "yes," because I choose
    to spare him that.

The Yellow Dog

It was a little yellow dog, a wistful thing to see,
A homely, skinny, battered pup, as dirty as could be;
His ribs were showing through his hide, his coat was
    thick with mud,
And yet the way he wagged his tail completely cap-
    tured Bud.

He had been kicked from door to door and stoned
    upon his way,
"Begone!" was all he'd ever heard, 'twas all that
    folks would say;

And yet this miserable cur, forever doomed to roam,
Struck up a comradeship with Bud, who proudly
brought him home.

I've never seen so poor a dog in all my stretch of
years,
The burrs were thick upon his tail and thick upon his
ears;
He'd had to fight his way through life and carried
many a scar,
But still Bud brought him home and cried: "Say, can
I keep him, Ma?"

I think the homeless terrier knows that age is harsh
and stern,
And from the shabby things of life in scorn is quick
to turn;
And when some scrubby yellow dog needs sympathy
and joy,
He's certain of a friend in need, if he can find a boy.

The Letter

The postman whistled down the street
And seemed to walk on lighter feet,
And as he stepped inside her gate
He knew he carried precious freight;
He knew that day he carried joy—
He had the letter from her boy.

Day after day he'd kept his pace
And seen her careworn, gentle face.
She watched for him to come and took
The papers with an anxious look,
But disappointment followed hope—
She missed the one glad envelope.

He stopped to chat with her awhile
And saw the sadness of her smile.
He fancied he could hear her sigh
The morning that he traveled by;
He knew that when to-morrow came
She would be waiting just the same.

The boy who was so far away
Could never hear her gently say:
"Well, have you brought good news to me?"
Her eager face he could not see,
Or note the lines of anxious care
As every day she waited there.

But when he wrote, on lighter feet
The happy postman walked the street.
"Well, here it is, at last," he'd shout,
"To end the worry and the doubt."
The robin on the maple limb
Began to sing: "She's heard from him."

Her eyes with joy began to glow,
The neighbors round her seemed to know

That with the postman at the door
Sweet peace had come to her once more.
When letters bring so much delight,
Why do the sons forget to write?

My Goals

A little braver when the skies are gray,
  A little stronger when the road seems long,
A little more of patience through the day,
  And not so quick to magnify a wrong.

A little kinder, both of thought and deed,
  A little gentler with the old and weak,
Swifter to sense another's pressing need,
  And not so fast the hurtful phrase to speak.

These are my goals—not flung beyond my power,
  Not dreams of glory, beautiful but vain,
Not the great heights where buds of genius flower,
  But simple splendors which I ought to gain.

These I can do and be from day to day
  Along the humble pathway where I plod,
So that at last when I am called away
  I need not make apologies to God.

The First Step

Last night she hurried out to say:
"The baby took a step to-day!"
A step alone!   Those little feet
Walked out two waiting hands to greet;

Walked boldly out, and left the chair
Which little hands had clung to there,
A very glorious hint to make
Of many steps she soon will take.

At eve they hurried out to say:
"The baby took a step to-day!"
What mattered letters, friendly calls,
And all the care which daily falls,
The news by 'phone, the gossip heard?
One thing important had occurred,
One big deed swept all else away:
The baby took a step to-day!

The baby took a step.   Ah, me!
The first of millions that will be!
Those little feet will walk and climb
And run along the road of Time;
They've started out, and where they'll go
'Tis not permitted us to know.
Out of her arms she turns away—
The baby took a step to-day!

Dear Lord, now hear me as I pray.
Our baby took a step to-day!

Grant that her little feet shall find
No cruel pathways or unkind.
Be Thou her guide through life, that she
May walk in safe security.
Let love and beauty light her way—
Our baby took a step to-day!

Failure

Failure is ceasing to try!
   'Tis accepting defeat
   And to all you may meet
Giving voice to a sigh;
'Tis in thinking it vain
   To attempt furthermore
And in bowing to pain
   When the muscles grow sore.

Failure is stepping aside
   From the brunt of the fray
   In a weak-hearted way,
Being content to abide
In the shadows that fall,
   And in being afraid
Out of life, after all,
   Nothing's left to be made.

Failure is thinking despair,
   The forsaking of hope,

And refusal to cope
With the day's round of care.
It's in heeding the cry,
    "All is lost!" and to stay
With defeat and not try
    For the happier day.

Baby Feet

Tell me, what is half so sweet
As a baby's tiny feet,
Pink and dainty as can be,
Like a coral from the sea?
Talk of jewels strung in rows,
Gaze upon those little toes,
Fairer than a diadem,
With the mother kissing them!

It is morning and she lies
Uttering her happy cries,
While her little hands reach out
For the feet that fly about.
Then I go to her and blow
Laughter out of every toe;
Hold her high and let her place
Tiny footprints on my face.

Little feet that do not know
Where the winding roadways go,

Little feet that never tire,
Feel the stones or trudge the mire,
Still too pink and still too small
To do anything but crawl,
Thinking all their wanderings fair,
Filled with wonders everywhere.

Little feet, so rich with charm,
May you never come to harm.
As I bend and proudly blow
Laughter out of every toe,
This I pray, that God above
Shall protect you with His love,
And shall guide those little feet
Safely down life's broader street.

"Wait Till Your Pa Comes Home"

"Wait till your Pa comes home!"   Oh, dear!
What a dreadful threat for a boy to hear.
Yet never a boy of three or four
But has heard it a thousand times or more.
"Wait till your Pa comes home, my lad,
And see what you'll get for being bad.

"Wait till your Pa comes home, you scamp!
You've soiled the walls with your fingers damp,
You've tracked the floor with your muddy feet
And fought with the boy across the street;

You've torn your clothes and you look a sight!
But wait till your Pa comes home to-night."

Now since I'm the Pa of that daily threat
Which paints me as black as a thing of jet
I rise in protest right here to say
I won't be used in so fierce a way;
No child of mine in the evening gloam
Shall be afraid of my coming home.

I want him waiting for me at night
With eyes that glisten with real delight;
When it's right that punished my boy should be
I don't want the job postponed for me;
I want to come home to a round of joy
And not to frighten a little boy.

"Wait till your Pa comes home!"   Oh, dear,
What a dreadful threat for a boy to hear.
Yet that is ever his Mother's way
Of saving herself from a bitter day;
And well she knows in the evening gloam
He won't be hurt when his Pa comes home.

Women Who Bait Fish Hooks

With rather dubious eyes I look
On women who can bait a hook,
And never squeal or never squirm
Impaling minnow or a worm.

A minnow, slippery and cold,
Seems such a slimy thing to hold,
That I've the ancient notion it's
A job to give a woman fits.

I know there's many a girl who can
Bait hooks as well as any man,
But just the same I seem to feel
That angle worms should make her squeal.

I do not criticise the kind
Of maid who man's work doesn't mind;
I'm just old fashioned and I look
Surprised to see one bait a hook.

Little Girls

God made the little boys for fun, for rough and
tumble times of play;
He made their little legs to run and race and scamper
through the day.
He made them strong for climbing trees, he suited
them for horns and drums,
And filled them full of revelries so they could be their
father's chums.
But then He saw that gentle ways must also travel
from above.
And so, through all our troubled days He sent us little
girls to love.

He knew that earth would never do, unless a bit of
    Heaven it had.
Men needed eyes divinely blue to toil by day and still
    be glad.
A world where only men and boys made merry would
    in time grow stale,
And so He shared His Heavenly joys that faith in
    Him should never fail.
He sent us down a thousand charms, He decked our
    ways with golden curls
And laughing eyes and dimpled arms. He let us
    have His little girls.

They are the tenderest of His flowers, the little angels
    of His flock,
And we may keep and call them ours, until God's
    messenger shall knock.
They bring to us the gentleness and beauty that we
    sorely need;
They soothe us with each fond caress and strengthen
    us for every deed.
And happy should that mortal be whom God has
    trusted, through the years,
To guard a little girl and see that she is kept from
    pain and tears.

Castor Oil

I don't mind lickin's, now an' then,
An' I can even stand it when

My mother calls me in from play
To run some errand right away.
There's things 'bout bein' just a boy
That ain't all happiness an' joy,
But I suppose I've got to stand
My share o' trouble in this land,
An' I ain't kickin' much—but, say,
The worst of parents is that they
Don't realize just how they spoil
A feller's life with castor oil.

Of all the awful stuff, Gee Whiz!
That is the very worst there is.
An' every time if I complain,
Or say I've got a little pain,
There's nothing else that they can think
'Cept castor oil for me to drink.
I notice, though, when Pa is ill,
That he gets fixed up with a pill,
An' Pa don't handle Mother rough
An' make her swallow nasty stuff;
But when I've got a little ache,
It's castor oil I've got to take.

I don't mind goin' up to bed
Afore I get the chapter read;
I don't mind bein' scolded, too,
For lots of things I didn't do;
But, Gee! I hate it when they say,
"Come! Swallow this—an' right away!"

Let poets sing about the joy
It is to be a little boy,
I'll tell the truth about my case:
The poets here can have my place,
An' I will take their life of toil
If they will take my castor oil.

I Don't Want to Go to Bed

World wide over this is said:
"I don't want to go to bed."
Dads and mothers, far and near,
Every night this chorus hear;
Makes no difference where they are,
Here or off in Zanzibar,
In the igloos made of snow
Of the fur-clad Eskimo,
In the blistering torrid zone,
This one touch of nature's known;
In life's various tongues it's said:
"I don't want to go to bed!"

This has ever been the way
Of the youngsters at their play.
Laughter quickly dries their tears,
Trouble swiftly disappears,
Joy is everywhere about,
Here and there and in and out;
Yet when night comes on they cry
That so glad a day should die,

And they think that they will miss
Something more of precious bliss,
So shouts every curly-head:
"I don't want to go to bed!"

Age is glad to put away
All the burdens of the day,
Glad to lay the worries down,
Quit the noises of the town,
And in slumber end the care
That has met them here and there.
But the children do not know
Life is freighted down with woe;
They would run until they drop,
Hoping day would never stop,
Calling back when it has fled:
"I don't want to go to bed."

Always Saying "Don't!"

Folks are queer as they can be,
Always sayin' "don't" to me;
Don't do this an' don't do that.
Don't annoy or tease the cat,
Don't throw stones, or climb a tree,
Don't play in the road. Oh, Gee!
Seems like when I want to play
"Don't" is all that they can say.

If I start to have some fun,
Someone hollers, "Don't you run!"

If I want to go an' play
Mother says: "Don't go away."
Seems my life is filled clear through
With the things I mustn't do.
All the time I'm shouted at:
"No, no, Sonny, don't do that!"

Don't shout so an' make a noise,
Don't play with those naughty boys,
Don't eat candy, don't eat pie,
Don't you laugh and don't you cry,
Don't stand up and don't you fall,
Don't do anything at all.
Seems to me both night an' day
"Don't" is all that they can say.

When I'm older in my ways
An' have little boys to raise,
Bet I'll let 'em race an' run
An' not always spoil their fun;
I'll not tell 'em all along
Everything they like is wrong;
An' you bet your life I won't
All the time be sayin' "don't."

No Children!

No children in the house to play—
It must be hard to live that way!

I wonder what the people do
When night comes on and the work is through,
With no glad little folks to shout,
No eager feet to race about,
No youthful tongues to chatter on
About the joy that's been and gone?
The house might be a castle fine,
But what a lonely place to dine!

No children in the house at all,
No fingermarks upon the wall,
No corner where the toys are piled—
Sure indication of a child.
No little lips to breathe the prayer
That God shall keep you in His care,
No glad caress and welcome sweet
When night returns you to your street;
No little lips a kiss to give—
Oh, what a lonely way to live!

No children in the house! I fear
We could not stand it half a year.
What would we talk about at night,
Plan for and work with all our might,
Hold common dreams about and find
True union of heart and mind,
If we two had no greater care
Than what we both should eat and wear?
We never knew love's brightest flame
Until the day the baby came.

And now we could not get along
Without their laughter and their song.
Joy is not bottled on a shelf,
It cannot feed upon itself;
And even love, if it shall wear,
Must find its happiness in care;
Dull we'd become of mind and speech
Had we no little ones to teach.
No children in the house to play!
Oh, we could never live that way!

My Paw Said So

Foxes can talk if you know how to listen,
    My Paw said so.
Owls have big eyes that sparkle an' glisten,
    My Paw said so.
Bears can turn flip-flaps an' climb ellum trees,
An' steal all the honey away from the bees,
An' they never mind winter becoz they don't freeze;
    My Paw said so.

Girls is a-scared of a snake, but boys ain't,
    My Paw said so.
They holler an' run; an' sometimes they faint,
    My Paw said so.
But boys would be 'shamed to be frightened that way
When all that the snake wants to do is to play:
You've got to believe every word that I say,
    My Paw said so.

Wolves ain't so bad if you treat 'em all right,
    My Paw said so.
They're as fond of a game as they are of a fight,
    My Paw said so.
An' all of the animals found in the wood
Ain't always ferocious.   Most times they are good.
The trouble is mostly they're misunderstood,
    My Paw said so.

You can think what you like, but I stick to it when
    My Paw said so.
An' I'll keep right on sayin', again an' again,
    My Paw said so.
Maybe foxes don't talk to such people as you,
An' bears never show you the tricks they can do,
But I know that the stories I'm tellin' are true,
    My Paw said so.

A Boy and His Dad

A boy and his dad on a fishing-trip—
There is a glorious fellowship!
Father and son and the open sky
And the white clouds lazily drifting by,
And the laughing stream as it runs along
With the clicking reel like a martial song,
And the father teaching the youngster gay
How to land a fish in the sportsman's way.

I fancy I hear them talking there
In an open boat, and the speech is fair;

And the boy is learning the ways of men
From the finest man in his youthful ken.
Kings, to the youngster, cannot compare
With the gentle father who's with him there.
And the greatest mind of the human race
Not for one minute could take his place.

Which is happier, man or boy?
The soul of the father is steeped in joy,
For he's finding out, to his heart's delight,
That his son is fit for the future fight.
He is learning the glorious depths of him,
And the thoughts he thinks and his every whim,
And he shall discover, when night comes on,
How close he has grown to his little son.

A boy and his dad on a fishing-trip—
Oh, I envy them, as I see them there
Under the sky in the open air,
For out of the old, old long-ago
Come the summer days that I used to know,
When I learned life's truths from my father's lips
As I shared the joy of his fishing-trips—
Builders of life's companionship!

Couldn't Live without You

You're just a little fellow with a lot of funny ways,
Just three-foot-six of mischief set with eyes that
    fairly blaze;

You're always up to something with those busy
      hands o' yours,
And you leave a trail o' ruin on the walls an' on the
      doors,
An' I wonder, as I watch you, an' your curious tricks
      I see,
Whatever is the reason that you mean so much to me.

You're just a chubby rascal with a grin upon your
      face,
Just seven years o' gladness, an' a hard an' trying
      case ;
You think the world's your playground, an' in all
      you say an' do
You fancy everybody ought to bow an' scrape to you ;
Dull care's a thing you laugh at just as though 'twill
      never be,
So I wonder, little fellow, why you mean so much
      to me.

Now your face is smeared with candy or perhaps
      it's only dirt,
An' it's really most alarming how you tear your little
      shirt ;
But I have to smile upon you, an' with all your wilful
      ways,
I'm certain that I need you 'round about me all my
      days ;
Yes, I've got to have you with me for somehow it's
      come to be
That I couldn't live without you, for you're all the
      world to me.

Aw Gee Whiz!

Queerest little chap he is,
Always saying: "Aw Gee Whiz!"
Needing something from the store
That you've got to send him for
And you call him from his play,
Then it is you hear him say:
    "Aw Gee Whiz!"

Seems that most expressive phrase
Is a part of childhood days;
Call him in at supper time,
Hands and face all smeared with grime,
Send him up to wash, and he
Answers you disgustedly:
    "Aw Gee Whiz!"

When it's time to go to bed
And he'd rather play instead,
As you call him from the street,
He comes in with dragging feet,
Knowing that he has to go,
Then it is he mutters low:
    "Aw Gee Whiz!"

Makes no difference what you ask
Of him as a little task;
He has yet to learn that life
Crosses many a joy with strife,

So when duty mars his play,
Always we can hear him say:
"Aw Gee Whiz!"

Story Telling

Most every night when they're in bed,
And both their little prayers have said,
They shout for me to come upstairs
And tell them tales of grizzly bears,
And Indians and gypsies bold,
And eagles with the claws that hold
A baby's weight, and fairy sprites
That roam the woods on starry nights.

And I must illustrate these tales,
Must imitate the northern gales
That toss the Indian's canoe,
And show the way he paddles, too.
If in the story comes a bear,
I have to pause and sniff the air
And show the way he climbs the trees
To steal the honey from the bees.

And then I buzz like angry bees
And sting him on his nose and knees
And howl in pain, till mother cries:
"That pair will never shut their eyes,
While all that noise up there you make;
You're simply keeping them awake."

And then they whisper: "Just one more,"
And once again I'm forced to roar.

New stories every night they ask,
And that is not an easy task;
I have to be so many things:
The frog that croaks, the lark that sings,
The cunning fox, the frightened hen;
But just last night they stumped me, when
They wanted me to twist and squirm
And imitate an angleworm.

At last they tumbled off to sleep,
And softly from their room I creep
And brush and comb the shock of hair
I tossed about to be a bear.
Then mother says: "Well, I should say
You're just as much a child as they."
But you can bet I'll not resign
That story-telling job of mine.

Constancy

When strange philosophers declare
The dismal doctrines of despair,
Walk round your garden and behold
The constancy of marigold.

Is it by chance from year to year
That blossoms fade and reappear?

That older than is history old
Are phlox and yellow marigold?

Is there a purpose to the plan
For garden flowers and not for man?
Do chrysalis and butterfly
Continue on and mortals die?

When order fails and spring no more
Brings the red robin to my door;
When stars run riot in the sky
I'll think that man was born to die.

A Sense of Humor

"What shall I give him now?" said God.
"He has the strength with which to plod
The ways of life, the love of right,
The gift of song when the skies are bright.

"Wisdom is planted in his mind,
This man shall be both true and kind,
Earth's beauty shall delight his eyes
And to its glories he shall rise.

"He shall know right from wrong, and he
Defender of the faith shall be;
What more on him can I bestow
Before to earth I let him go?"

Then spake an angel standing near:
"Wisdom is not enough, I fear,
Master, for all that he must do—
Grant him a sense of humor, too.

"Grant him to smile at petty wrong,
The changing moods which sway the throng;
When cares annoy him, show him then
How laughable are angry men!"

Years after, when his strength was tasked,
"What keeps you patient?" he was asked,
"What keeps you brave who are so tried?"
"My sense of humor," he replied.

Imagination

The dreamer sees the finished thing before the start
    is made;
He sees the roses pink and red beyond the rusty
    spade,
And all that bleak and barren spot which is so bare
    to see
Is but a place where very soon the marigolds will be.

Imagination carries him across the dusty years,
And what is dull and commonplace in radiant charm
    appears.

The little home that he will build where willows bend
    and bow
Is but the dreamer's paper sketch, but he can see it
    now.

He sees the little winding walk that slowly finds his
    door,
The chimney in its ivy dress, the children on the
    floor,
The staircase where they'll race and romp, the win-
    dows where will gleam
The light of peace and happiness—the house that's
    still a dream.

You see but weeds and rubbish there, and ugliness
    and grime,
But he can show you where there'll be a swing in
    summer time.
And he can show you where there'll be a fireplace
    rich with cheer,
Although you stand and shake your head and think
    the dreamer queer.

Imagination! This it is the dreamer has to-day;
He sees the beauty that shall be when time has cleared
    the way.
He reads the blueprint of his years, and he can plainly
    see
Beyond life's care and ugliness—the joy that is to be.

The Face on the Barroom Floor
(Modern Version)

He walked into the cocktail room, a figure gaunt and
grim.
The ladies occupied the stools and left no room for
him.
He doffed his hat and looked about. The barkeep
muttered: "Scram!"
"I want a drink," the stranger said. "A thirsty man
I am.
Give me a shot of Bourbon, please. I'll take it in
a cup."
"Out!" said the barkeep, "out with you! You can't
drink standing up!"

"I've got a tale to tell," he said. The women gathered there
All turned to look upon the man, but no one left her
chair.
"I know you think it strange," said he, "to see a man
in here
Where all's so dainty and refined; but let me make
it clear:
I used to be a happy man before we got repeal,
But now I never know what time I'll get my evening
meal.

"I loved a girl named Madelon and beautiful was
she,
Before those Prohibition days her strongest drink
was tea."

Some of the ladies laughed outright. A grandma,
    more refined,
Emptied her cocktail glass and said: "Let's hear
    what's on his mind."
"I've searched the town for Madelon. She's some-
    where on the roam.
The children need their supper now, I want to take
    her home.

"I am an artist." From his coat a piece of chalk he
    fetched
And kneeling on the barroom floor a lovely face he
    sketched.
"There, that is Madelon!" he cried. The women
    turned to see.
"If she should drop in here tonight please send her
    home to me!"
He left the place without a drink. A lady fixed her
    hat
And said: "If I were Madelon I'd never stand for
    that!"

Prayer for the Home

Peace, unto this house, I pray,
Keep terror and despair away;
Shield it from evil and let sin
Never find lodging room within.
May never in these walls be heard
The hateful or accusing word.

Grant that its warm and mellow light
May be to all a beacon bright,
A flaming symbol that shall stir
The beating pulse of him or her
Who finds this door and seems to say,
"Here end the trials of the day."

Hold us together, gentle Lord,
Who sit about this humble board;
May we be spared the cruel fate
Of those whom hatreds separate;
Here let love bind us fast, that we
May know the joys of unity.

Lord, this humble house we'd keep
Sweet with play and calm with sleep.
Help us so that we may give
Beauty to the lives we live.
Let Thy love and let Thy grace
Shine upon our dwelling place.

Things Work Out

Because it rains when we wish it wouldn't,
Because men do what they often shouldn't,
Because crops fail, and plans go wrong—
Some of us grumble all day long.
But somehow, in spite of the care and doubt,
It seems at the last that things work out.

Because we lose where we hoped to gain,
Because we suffer a little pain,
Because we must work when we'd like to play—
Some of us whimper along life's way.
But somehow, as day always follows the night,
Most of our troubles work out all right.

Because we cannot forever smile,
Because we must trudge in the dust awhile,
Because we think that the way is long—
Some of us whimper that life's all wrong.
But somehow we live and our sky grows bright,
And everything seems to work out all right.

So bend to your trouble and meet your care,
For the clouds must break, and the sky grow fair.
Let the rain come down, as it must and will,
But keep on working and hoping still.
For in spite of the grumblers who stand about,
Somehow, it seems, all things work out.

The Good World

The Lord must have liked us, I say when I see
The bloom of the rose and the green of the tree,
The flash of the wing of a bird flitting by,
The gold of the grain and the blue of the sky,
The clover below and the tall pines above—
Oh, there's something about us the good Lord must
    love.

The Lord must have liked us, I say when I stand
Where the waves like an army come into the land,
With the gulls riding high on the crest of the breeze
And the ducks flying north in their echelon V's,
The sun slipping down into liquefied gold—
Oh, it's then the great love of the Lord I behold.

The Lord must have liked us, I say at the dawn
When the diamonds of dew gleam and glow on the
    lawn,
And the birds from their throats pour the red wine
    of song
As if life held no burden of sorrow or wrong;
The Lord must have loved us, I whisper just then,
To give such a world to the children of men.

The Lord must have liked us, I say as I pass
The nest of a meadow lark deep in the grass,
Or hear in the distance the quail calling clear
And know that his mate and his babies are near;
Oh, I say to myself as His wonders I see,
The Lord loves us all or this never would be.

A Thought

    Were I as rich as Midas
      Or poor as Lazarus,
  If love would walk beside us
    Together we'd discuss

A thousand lovely reasons
  For rapture and delight—
The ever-changing seasons,
  A wild duck's certain flight.

We'd sit the bright stars under
  And watch the moon arise,
And find it joy to wonder
  What lies beyond the skies;
We'd hear a blithe bird singing
  Its rhapsody of song,
And watch the rivers swinging
  Their seaward course along.

We'd hear the ocean booming
  Along the sandy shore,
And look at flowers, blooming
  Beside some humble door;
We'd gaze on green things growing
  And marvels everywhere
Beyond our little knowing
  And quite forget our care.

In spite of pain or duty,
  Or hearts that often ache,
We'd reap the joys of beauty
  Beyond man's power to make.
We'd find with love to guide us
  God's works miraculous,
Were I as rich as Midas
  Or poor as Lazarus.

The Effort

When man has done his level best,
   I fancy God is satisfied.
He need not be in splendor dressed,
Known north and south and east and west,
   Nor tread the paths of pride;
If he is earnest in the test,
   God knows how hard he tried.

Not all the good men rise to fame,
   Nor all the kings are crowned.
Full many a long forgotten name
Has borne life's battle but to claim
   An unremembered mound.
And men from men have suffered blame
   When God no fault has found.

'Tis fine to do the splendid deed,
   'Tis sweet to reach the goal.
But oft the dreams of men may lead
Them past their strength, to fall and bleed,
   And failure signs the scroll.
But 'tis not said we must succeed
   To make the perfect soul.

When man has done his level best,
   I fancy God is satisfied.
Though night shall find him sore distressed,
Beset by cares, by men oppressed,
   His victory denied,

God knows how cruel was the test
And just how hard he tried!

The Butterfly Discusses Evolution

"In a very recent age,"
    Said a wise and serious sage
To a butterfly with wings of golden flame,
    "You were not so fair to see,
    You've a horrid ancestry,
From a crawling caterpillar stock you came.

"Now you proudly spread your wings
    And you feed on dainty things,
You are beautiful to look at, but I shrug
    My shoulders with disdain,
    When I think how very plain
You must have been when you were but a slug."

Said the butterfly: "I know
    In some distant long ago
As a caterpillar crawling on my way,
    I was lowly as could be,
    But what is that to you or me?
I am certainly a butterfly to-day!

"As a caterpillar slow
    I could never guess or know
What my purpose was while crawling on the bough;

But I stretch my wings and fly,
And you surely can't deny
That I am a lovely butterfly right now!"

What Counts

It isn't the money you're making, it isn't the clothes
you wear,
And it isn't the skill of your good right hand which
makes folks really care.
It's the smile on your face and the light of your eye
and the burdens that you bear.

Most any old man can tell you, most any old man at
all,
Who has lived through all sorts of weather, winter
and summer and fall,
That riches and fame are shadows that dance on the
garden wall.

It's how do you live and neighbor, how do you work
and play,
It's how do you say "good morning" to the people
along the way,
And it's how do you face your troubles whenever
your skies are gray.

It's you, from the dawn to nighttime; you when the
day is fair,

You when the storm is raging—how do you face
    despair?
It is you that the world discovers, whatever the
    clothes you wear.

You to the end of the journey, kindly and brave and
    true,
The best and the worst of you gleaming in all that
    you say and do,
And the thing that counts isn't money, or glory or
    power, but *you!*

A Summer Day

Blue in the sky and green in the tree
And a bird singing anthems of gladness for me,
    A breeze soft and fair
    As a little girl's hair,
With nothing that's ugly or base anywhere;
    A world that's swept clean
    Of the doubtful and mean,
With nowhere a hint of the care that has been.

I stand at my gate with the sun in my face,
And I thank the good Lord for such beauty and
    grace.
    Time was, I declare
    When the snows drifted there,
And those boughs with their blossoms were ugly and
    bare.

Now the sin and the wrong
  Of the cold days and long
Are lost in life's splendor of sunshine and song.

God makes it all right in good time, I believe,
We doubt when we're troubled, we doubt when we
        grieve;
  Like a stark, barren tree
  Looms the wrong which we see.
Hurt, anguish and care hide the splendor to be,
  But at last from the pain
  Rises beauty again,
And there's never a bough that has suffered in vain.

Perhaps at the last, 'neath a lovelier sun,
When the anguish and hurt of life's growing is done,
  We may rise from our pain
  Showing never a stain
Of the cares of the years which fell on us like rain;
  When the soul is set free
  All the flaws we now see
May be lost in the joy of the new life to be.

Grace at Evening

For all the beauties of the day,
The innocence of childhood's play,
For health and strength and laughter sweet,
Dear Lord, our thanks we now repeat.

For this our daily gift of food
We offer now our gratitude,
For all the blessings we have known
Our debt of gratefulness we own.

Here at the table now we pray,
Keep us together down the way;
May this, our family circle, be
Held fast by love and unity.

Grant, when the shades of night shall fall,
Sweet be the dreams of one and all;
And when another day shall break
Unto Thy service may we wake.

Grandpa's Walking Stick

My grandpa once was very sick
And now he's got a walking stick,
Coz one of his legs, as he says to me,
Isn't quite so good as it used to be;
And he can't run and he daresen't kick
Coz he'd fall if he hadn't his walking stick.

When my grandpa comes to our house to stay
I like to carry his stick away,
And put it in places where he can't see,
Then he can't get up to come after me.
And he shouts out loud: "Hey! Everyone!
Who knows where my other leg has gone?

"I had it here by my chair and now
It's disappeared from its place somehow.
I'll bet this little Miss Mischief here
Knows something about it, she looks so queer.
Was it you, who carried my leg away?"
"Maybe 'twas eat by a bear," I say.

Then he can't get up and he can't move round
Till I come and tell him his leg is found.
The bear didn't swallow it after all,
He must have got frightened and let it fall.
Then my grandpa laughs till his sides are sore,
And we hippety-hop to the candy store.

Boyhood Memory

It used to be fun in the good old days to rise at the
    dawn of day
And dig for worms for a fishing trip. It used to be
    fun, I say,
For I'll swear that a robin who hovered near knew
    just what we were about,
Since he flew to the ground when the earth was
    turned and begged us to toss one out.
Yes, it used to be fun to go fishing then, but Time
    has rewritten my terms
Of what pleasure is, and I never get up to dig for a
    can of worms.

We'd sit on a dock and we'd swing our legs all day
    in the blazing sun,
And a few small fish on a piece of string was our
    ultimate dream of fun.
Then digging for worms was an easy task, but I tried
    it a year ago
And the earth seemed hard as a city street where the
    streams of traffic flow.
And I'd lost the knack of clutching a thing that
    wriggles and twists and squirms,
So I said to myself: "You will never again go dig-
    ging at dawn for worms."

I stuck to the task till my hands grew sore, I labored
    and toiled and wrought,
But the worms were scarce and no robins came, and
    it wasn't the fun I thought.
But a small boy said as we walked away: "I'm
    wondering, Uncle Ed,
When there's so much pleasure in getting up, how
    can old folks stay in bed?"
I could only answer him this: "My lad, all experience
    confirms
The dreadful fact that there comes a time when it's
    labor to dig for worms."

The Old Prospector Talks

Gold is found in the hills, and then
Carried back to the haunts of men.

And two of us came in the early days
To pan the streams for the dirt that pays.

And we stuck it out for a time, till he
Got sick of the game which enchanted me.
And he went back to the town one day
To get his gold in an easier way.

He quit these hills and he left me cold
To scramble with men for his bit of gold.
Now some like walls and roofs and rooms,
But I like mountains where thunder booms,

And skies and trees and the open plains
Where a man must work for the bit he gains.
So I've stayed right here and I've dreamed my dreams
And smoked my pipe by these running streams,

And kept my cabin up here alone,
With all this beauty to call my own.
I've taken my gold with pick and pan
And sent it back to be stained by man.

I've wrestled with rocks and streams for mine
And made my friendships with fir and pine.
Now the world down there may think me odd,
But maybe I won't seem queer to God.

The Old Hat

To-day as I was starting out,
The lady that I write about
Stood at the door as if to chat,
Then handed me an old-time hat,
A bonnet I had worn, I know,
The first time several years ago;
"Now get this cleaned," she said to me,
"And just as good as new 'twill be."

I chuckled as I carried down
That old fedora, rusty brown.
I chuckled, living that scene o'er,
The good wife standing at the door,
As earnest as a wife can be,
Handing that worn-out lid to me,
And saying: "Have this cleaned, my dear,
'Twill serve you for another year."

Let's twist the scene around and see
What would occur if I should be
Prompted to try a trick like that
And hand to her an ancient hat,
A bonnet of a vintage rare,
Saying: "It's good enough to wear
Just have this blocked and cleaned, my dear,
'Twill serve you for another year."

I fancy then the fur would fly
If such a trick I dared to try.

She'd wither me with looks of scorn
And spoil another autumn morn.
But let it drop. A man and wife
Have different views of hats and life,
And meekly to the Greek I went
And had it cleaned—and she's content.

Loser and Victor

He was beaten from the start,
Beaten by his doubting heart,
And he had a ready ear
For the busy tongue of fear,
And he had a timid mind
Unto fretfulness inclined,
Filled with many reasons why
It was vain for him to try.

Given a task he'd shake his head,
"Can't do that!" he often said,
"Times are hard and none will stay,
Listening to the words I say.
It is futile now to try.
People simply will not buy!"
Thus he walked the streets of trade,
Both discouraged and afraid.

But another kind of man
Thought this way: "Perhaps I can!
If I will supply the pluck,
Fortune may provide the luck.

If I have the grit to try,
There are people who may buy;
Anyhow, I'll not submit
To defeat before I'm hit."

One was beaten from the start,
Beaten by his doubting heart,
Beaten when he gave his ear
To the busy tongue of fear.
But another with his chance
Seized the moment to advance,
And came happy home at night
Just because he dared to fight.

The Little Home

The little house is not too small
To shelter friends who come to call.
Though low the roof and small its space
It holds the Lord's abounding grace,
And every simple room may be
Endowed with happy memory.

The little house, severely plain,
A wealth of beauty may contain.
Within it those who dwell may find
High faith which makes for peace of mind,
And that sweet understanding which
Can make the poorest cottage rich.

The little house can hold all things
From which the soul's contentment springs.
'Tis not too small for love to grow,
For all the joys that mortals know,
For mirth and song and that delight
Which makes the humblest dwelling bright.

Merit and the Throng

A thousand men filed in by day
To work and later draw their pay;
A thousand men with hopes and dreams,
Ambitions, visions, plans and schemes.
And in the line a youth who said:
"What chance have I to get ahead?
In such a throng, can any tell
Whether or not I labor well?"

Yet merit is so rare a trait
That once it enters by the gate,
Although 'tis mingled with the throng,
The news of it is passed along.
A workman sees a willing boy,
And talks about his find with joy;
A foreman hears the word, and seeks
The lad of whom another speaks.

So up the line the news is passed,
And to the chief it comes at last.

A willing ear to praise he lends,
Then for that eager boy he sends
And gives him little tasks to do
To learn if all that's said be true.
Among the throng the lad is one
He keeps a watchful eye upon.

Oh, youngster, walking with the throng,
Although to-day the road seems long,
Remember that it lies with you
To say what kind of work you'll do.
If you are only passing fair
The chief will never know you're there,
But if you've merit, have no doubt,
The chief will quickly find it out.

A Few New Teeth

The dentist tinkered day by day,
    With wax and sticky gum;
He built a model out of clay
    And shaped it with his thumb.
He made the man a lovely plate,
    With three teeth in a row,
And bars of gold to keep them straight,
    Then said: "They'll never show.

"Go forth," the dentist told the man,
    "As proud as you can be.
Those teeth are perfect. No one can
    Tell they were bought from me.

Why I, by whom the work was wrought,
  The truth had never known.
Were you a stranger I'd have thought
  Those teeth were all your own."

While going out he bumped a miss.
  "Excuthe me pleathe," he said.
The lady smiled to hear him hiss—
  His cheeks went flaming red.
He met a friend upon the street,
  Who joined him for a walk
And said: "Let's go where we can eat,
  And have a quiet talk."

"I'd rather walk," the man exclaimed.
  "Leth thtay upon the threet,
For with you I thould be athamed
  Thum tholid food to eat."
"New teeth?" the friend remarked, and low
  The troubled man said: "Yeth!
My dentith thwore you'd never know.
  However did you guetth?"

Dreams

One broken dream is not the end of dreaming,
  One shattered hope is not the end of all,
Beyond the storm and tempest stars are gleaming,
  Still build your castles, though your castles fall.

Though many dreams come tumbling in disaster,
  And pain and heartache meet us down the years,
Still keep your faith, your dreams and hopes to
      master
  And seek to find the lesson of your tears.

Not all is as it should be! See how littered
  With sorry wreckage is life's restless stream.
Some dreams are vain, but be you not embittered
  And never cry that you have ceased to dream!

"I Didn't Think" and "I Forgot"

The weakest excuses of all the lot
Are: "I didn't think" and "I forgot."
Worn and weary and haggered and pale,
They follow the path of the men who fail—
In thread-bare raiment from place to place
They've dogged the steps of the human race.
In most of the blunders which men have made
This pitiful pair a part have played.

A man cries out on disaster's brink:
"I should have stopped but I didn't think!"
Was the barn door locked last night? 'Twas not.
And somebody mutters: "Oh, I forgot!"
Since Adam and Eve and the world began,
This pair have followed the trail of man.
The commonest phrases in printer's ink
Are "I forgot" and "I didn't think."

Yet man will think if a pleasure calls,
And there isn't a doubt that he recalls
The promise another has made to him;
And a boy will think that he wants to swim,
And the chances are that he won't forget
That he mustn't come home with his hair all wet.
It's strange, but duty is all I find
That ever escapes from a failure's mind.

Search the burdens which men must bear
And you'll find the tracks of this precious pair.
With needless trouble this world they've filled,
And who can measure the tears they've spilled?
"I forgot" has wrecked ship and train,
"I didn't think" has caused endless pain,
And God must smile, as He sees us sink,
At our "I forgot" and "I didn't think."

Had Youth Been Willing to Listen

If youth had been willing to listen
    To all that its grandfathers told,
If the gray-bearded sage by the weight of his age
    Had been able attention to hold,
We'd be reading by candles and heating with wood,
And where we were then we'd have certainly stood.

If youth had been willing to listen
    To the warnings and hints of the wise,
Had it taken as true all the best which they knew,
    And believed that no higher we'd rise,

The windows of sick rooms would still be kept shut
And we'd still use a cobweb to bandage a cut.

If youth had been willing to listen,
  Had it clung to the best of the past,
With oxen right now we'd be struggling to plough
  And thinking a horse travels fast.
We'd have stood where we were beyond question or
      doubt
If some pestilent germ hadn't wiped us all out.

So, although I am gray at the temples,
  And settled and fixed in my ways,
I wouldn't hold youth to the limits of truth
  That I learned in my brief yesterdays.
And I say to myself as they come and they go:
"Those kids may find something this age doesn't
      know."

The Cynic

In all this world of loveliness there lies
Some blemish to attract the cynic's eyes;
The rose of June is born of ache and hurt;
The cynic says: "Its roots are in the dirt."

A little child comes racing down the street;
The cynic says: " 'Twill grow to be a cheat."
Ground for a hospital a rich man buys;
The cynic jeers: "It pays to advertise."

Honor is doubted, mercy a mistake.
The marriage vow is only made to break;
The cheerful neighbor is a grinning fool,
And only idiots live by law and rule.

Yet youth goes blithely singing on its way,
And men and women brave the heat of day,
Finding life's beauty worth its cost in tears;
And joy exists, despite the cynic's sneers.

The Fool

I'm the sort of a fool that will pull up a chair,
And then let a child come and rumple his hair,
And climb on his stomach and wiggle about,
Go through his pockets and empty them out,
And say when such mischievous rompings are done:
"Well, wasn't it fun?"

I'm the sort of a fool that will settle to read
A book, or a paper, a tract, or a screed,
And then let a blue-eyed and plump little maid,
Who of nobody living seems ever afraid,
Come right up and snatch what I'm reading away
Shouting: "Come, let us play!"

I'm the sort of a fool that will calmly sit by,
While a cute little finger is poked in his eye,
And a cute little foot kicks him square in the front
So hard that the neighbors are shocked at his grunt,

And then say with a grin when the fooling is done,
"Well, wasn't it fun!"

Counting the Babies

How many babies have you?
Well, really we've more than a few!
We've little Miss Laughter
And little Miss Pout,
And then there is little
Miss Scamperabout;
I never have counted them, good, bad and fair,
For the number is constantly changing I swear.

We've babies too many to tell,
We've little Miss Arrogant Belle,
We've little Miss Mischief
And little Miss Bold,
We've little Miss Whimper
And little Miss Scold.
And little Miss Hunger, who gets in the way,
Begging for cookies each hour of the day.

You'd not see them all in a week,
There's the bashful and little Miss Meek.
We've little Miss Blue Eyes
And little Miss Don't,
And that dreadful and
Troublesome little Miss Won't!
And the one that's as grasping as misers can be,
I refer to our little Miss Give It To Me!

I wish all their names that I knew,
There's little Miss Take Off Her Shoe.
There's little Miss Tippy-toe,
Little Miss Clutch,
Little Miss Sticky-thumbs,
Ruining much,
We've little Miss Drowsy, but need I keep on?
We've every known baby, and yet we've but one!

To a Little Girl

Little girl, just half-past three,
Take this little rhyme from me,
All the joy that gold can bring,
All the songs the birds can sing,
All this world can hold to give
Grown-up men the while they live.
Hath not half the charm of you
And the lovely things you do.

Little girl, just half-past three,
When God sent you down to me
Oft I wonder, did He know
Fortune's power would dwindle so?
Did He know that I should find
Such a curious change of mind,
And should some day come to see
Just how trivial pomp can be?

Little girl, just half-past three,
Lost are dreams that used to be.

Now the things I thought worth while
Could not buy your lovely smile,
And I would not give you up
For the golden plate and cup
And the crown a king may boast.
In my life you're uppermost.

Little girl, just half-past three,
This is what you mean to me,
More than all that money buys,
More than any selfish prize,
More than fortune, more than fame,
And I learned this when you came.
Other fathers know it, too.
Nothing matters more than you.

A Dog

'Tis pity not to have a dog,
    For at the long day's end
The man or boy will know the joy
    Of welcome from a friend.
And whether he be rich or poor
    Or much or little bring,
The dog will mark his step and bark
    As if he were a king.

Though gossips whisper now and then
    Of faults they plainly see,
And some may sneer, from year to year
    My dog stays true to me.

He's glad to follow where I go,
   And though I win or fail
His love for me he'll let me see
   By wagging of his tail.

Now if I were to list the friends
   Of mine in smiles and tears
Who through and through are staunch
     and true
   And constant down the years,
In spite of all my many faults
   Which critics catalog
Deserving blame, I'd have to name
   My ever-faithful dog.

'Tis pity not to have a dog,
   Whatever be his breed,
For dogs possess a faithfulness
   Which humans sadly need.
And whether skies be blue or gray,
   Good luck or ill attend
Man's toil by day, a dog will stay
   His ever-constant friend.

The Home

Write it down that here I labored,
Here I sang and laughed and neighbored;
Here's the sum of all my story,
Here's my fortune and my glory;

These four walls and friendly door
Mark the goal I struggled for.
Never mind its present worth,
Here's one hundred feet of earth
Where the passer-by can see
Every dream which came to me.

Write it down: my life uncloses
Here among these budding roses;
In this patch of lawn I've tended,
Here is all I've counted splendid;
Here's the goal that's held me true
To the tasks I've had to do.
Here for all the world to scan
Is my secret thought and plan;
Through the long years gone before,
This is what I struggled for.

Write it down, when I have perished:
Here is everything I've cherished;
That these walls should glow with beauty
Spurred my lagging soul to duty;
That there should be gladness here
Kept me toiling, year by year.
Here in phlox and marigold
Is my every purpose told;
Every thought and every act
Were to keep this home intact.

Myself

I have to live with myself, and so
I want to be fit for myself to know;
I want to be able as days go by
Always to look myself straight in the eye;
I don't want to stand with the setting sun
And hate myself for the things I've done.

I don't want to keep on a closet shelf
A lot of secrets about myself,
And fool myself as I come and go
Into thinking that nobody else will know
The kind of a man I really am;
I don't want to dress myself up in sham.

I want to go out with my head erect,
I want to deserve all men's respect;
But here in the struggle for fame and pelf,
I want to be able to like myself.
I don't want to think as I come and go
That I'm bluster and bluff and empty show.

I never can hide myself from me,
I see what others may never see,
I know what others may never know,
I never can fool myself—and so,
Whatever happens, I want to be
Self-respecting and conscience free.

Sunset

Some days die, as some men,
Softly and peacefully, and then
Others with pain-wracked twisted forms
Go to their graves 'mid gales and storms,
And knowing only skies of gray
And the wind's weird wail they pass away.

I watched the death of yesterday.
Golden the couch on which it lay.
Imperial purple edged a cloud
As if it were a monarch's shroud,
And there was neither pain nor fright
To mar the silence of the night.

Beauty and glory watched beside
The old day's bed until it died.
Troops robed in scarlet seemed to stay
To bear the noble corpse away,
Then hooded dusk with footsteps slow
Lighted night's candles, row by row.

Lord, for my loved ones, this I pray:
Sweet be the sunset of their day!
May beauty grace their lives, and when
Thou call'st their spirits home again
May trails of glory round them sweep
As silently they fall asleep.

Hand in Hand

All the way to age we'll go
    Hand in hand together;
All the way to brows of snow
    Through every sort of weather.
Rain or shine, blue sky or gray,
    Joy and sorrow sharing
Hand in hand along the way
    We'll go bravely faring.

All the way to sunset land
    We'll walk down together
Side by side and hand in hand
    Held by Cupid's tether.
Once we danced in early May
    Steps we'll long remember;
So we'll trip the miles away
    Even to December.

Let the years go fleeting by!
    Gray old age shall find us
Still recalling smile and sigh
    Long since left behind us.
And though feeble we may grow,
    Worn by wind and weather,
All the way to Age we'll go
    Hand in hand together.

Barabbas

Barabbas, convicted of murder; Barabbas, the ne'er-
    do-well,
Awaiting the death of a felon, sat in his prison cell.
Already his cross was fashioned—at dawn they
    would nail him high;
When down through the dingy cell house there came
    to his ears a cry:

"Barabbas! Barabbas! Barabbas! Barabbas whose
    hands are red!
Take you the lowly Nazarene's and spare us his life
    instead."
And a sickened and frightened Pilate who dared not
    their pleas deny
Released to the mob Barabbas and ordered the Christ
    to die.

They saved him with shout and tumult, Barabbas
    with hands unclean,
Barabbas, of evil doing, who knew not the Nazarene,
Was saved by a sudden fancy, turned loose and not
    knowing why—
Sent back to the street and the gutter, alone and un-
    loved, to die.

In the gloom of that gray Good Friday the Saviour
    they crucified,
And the mad throng stood about Him and mocked
    till the hour He died;

They knew not what they were doing, but Pilate,
     pale and afraid,
Stood at the window watching, regretting the choice
     they'd made!

Money

Does money bring men gladness?
     Yes, at times!
It also brings men sadness
     And to crimes.

Earned well it is a pleasure,
     None denies;
But in the love of treasure
     Danger lies.

Who grasps for it in blindness,
     Foul or fair,
Sells out to bleak unkindness
     And despair.

By money friends are parted;
     Hatred sown;
For money, marble-hearted,
     Men have grown.

Money's important. All require it
     Till life is o'er,
But it destroys men who desire it
     And nothing more.

William Comes Courting

William comes a-courting,
  And smiles his best on me;
His happiest behavior
  Is offered me to see,
His eyes are bright with smiling,
  He speaks a glad hello,
And asks me how I'm feeling,
  As if he cared to know.

When William comes a-courting
  He stands, with courteous air,
Until I say: "Be seated,"
  And offer him a chair.
He asks about my business
  And talks of all the news.
When William comes a-courting
  I think he'd shine my shoes.

When William comes a-courting
  It's plain as plain can be,
Although he wants my daughter
  He's also courting me.
And I just sit and chuckle
  To watch this hopeful lad,
For years ago, just like him,
  I worked on Nellie's dad.

The Second-hand Shop

There's a little old man in a little old shop
That is cluttered with things from the cellar to top.
There is something of everything scattered about,
But whatever you want, he can ferret it out.
"Now just wait a minute," he says with a grin,
"I'll find what you're after. It's somewhere within."

This second-hand store of this little old man
I drop in to visit whenever I can,
For he in himself is a lovely antique,
And there's something about him so gentle and meek
That, just like the trinkets he sells, it appears
He has taken on charm with the dust of the years.

I chuckle to see him go shuffling around
Till the treasure he seeks in the rubbish is found,
And I fancy sometimes, as I sit there and chat
In that jumble of things, that man's mind is like that.
It's a second-hand shop filled with good stuff and
	cheap,
Gathered down through the years and all tossed in a
	heap.

Man gathers the good and the bad as he goes;
What he has, where it is, it is he only knows.
The stranger who sees but the rags and the bones,
Looks in without finding the good thoughts he owns;
But buried beneath all the rubbish that's vile,
May be fancies and dreams that are very worth while.

Books

Upon my shelf they stand in rows,
   A city-full of human souls,
   Sages, philosophers and drolls—
Good friends that everybody knows.
   The drunkard shoulders with the saint;
   The great are neighboring with the quaint
And they will greet me one and all
At any hour I care to call.

There's Dickens with his humble crew
   That has no end of joy to give.
   With all his people I can live
By moving just a foot or two.
   Or should I choose to sail the sea,
   Stevenson there will pilot me,
While jovial, lovable Mark Twain
Waits patiently my call again.

Sometimes a friend drops in and looks
   My little sitting room around
   And, in a manner most profound,
Remarks: "Your shelves are lined with books!"
   "Not books," I say, "but people wise
   And men to cling to or despise.
Vast peopled cities, calm and still;
For me to visit when I will."

Because He Stayed Humble

Because he loved the poor of purse
  And gave his hand to them,
The rich and proud who scorned the crowd
  Were prompted to condemn.
Because he often stopped to speak
  With people poorly clad
And sought to ease their miseries,
  The wise men thought him mad.

Because by purple robes and gold
  He was not much impressed,
But daily taught this simple thought
  That brotherhood is best,
The men who fancied wisdom lies
  Alone in ancient lores,
With faces grim looked down on him
  And drove him from their doors.

Because he knew and understood
  The heartaches of the throng
And with them walked and freely talked
  Great statesmen thought him wrong.
Because he said the joys of life
  And all that makes it good,
And peace at night were a common right,
  He died, misunderstood.

Because he chose to play the friend
  To those whose need was great

And liked to share a poor man's care
   He won a monarch's hate.
And still men worship pomp and power
   And thrust the meek aside,
Nor ever guess what friendliness
   Is lost through petty pride.

Suggestions for Men

She ordered her lunch, and then as she sat
At the table she took off her little blue hat,
Held up a mirror, as wide as a book,
And sideways and frontways proceeded to look;
She picked up a comb and she tossed back her hair,
She pulled it out here and she tucked it in there.
As I watched her I said to myself: "There's a hunch!
That's something to do while you're waiting for
    lunch!"

From a tube she squeezed stuff on her pink finger tips
And calmly proceeded to varnish her lips;
She penciled her eyebrows an ebony black,
And I wondered what else she could have in that
    sack;
She tinted her cheeks till they beggared the rose,
And the maid brought her food as she powdered her
    nose.
"Now there is a first-class idea," thought I,
"If the girls can do that why should men be so shy?"

Why doesn't somebody get out for a man
A neat little package, with soap in a can,
A razor, a brush and a looking-glass small,
So neat that his pocket could carry it all?
This is one of the sayings the classics produce,
"The sauce for the gander is sauce for the goose."
After ordering lunch, precious time could be saved
If, while waiting, he got out his razor and shaved.

Why not copy the women? 'Twould be no disgrace
For a man to be openly kind to his face.
With a neat pocket outfit like this I suggest,
Man could always contrive to appear at his best.
At noon time, on street cars, with moments to spare,
At the dentist's, while waiting his turn in the chair,
Or while dummy at bridge, unconcernedly grave,
He could take off his necktie and collar and shave.

Perfection

Bright and beautiful and gay
Twenty roses in bouquet,
Twenty roses, pink and white!
Where could be a prettier sight?
But an expert shook his head,
"Just one perfect bloom," he said.

"Most of these have suffered pain,
Borne the wind and felt the rain,

Struggled for existence, and
If a rose you understand
Closely scan them; you will see
Flaws and faults that shouldn't be.

"Here's the only perfect bloom
Of the twenty in the room,
See the petals, note the stem—
Just as God intended them;
All the rest, though fair to see,
Fail the finished rose to be."

"Since," thought I, "the perfect rose
Only very seldom grows,
Is it any wonder, then,
In this teeming world of men,
Swayed and torn by storms of care,
Perfect souls are very rare?"

The Fish That Gets Away

Some mourn the fish that gets away
    And boast his size and weight;
They stop their friends at night to say
    How sorry was their fate.
Almost unto the net they'd brought
    This beauty superfine;
It seemed to them they had him caught
    And then he snapped the line.

Oh, yes, they had some fish to show
　　For all the time they'd spent;
Some luck they'd been allowed to know,
　　But they were not content.
The ones they'd caught seemed rather small
　　When put upon display,
And could not be compared at all
　　With that which got away.

He broke but once where sunbeams dance
　　Upon the waters blue,
And though at him they'd but a glance
　　His weight and size they knew.
Not one in all their splendid catch,
　　Which came to them that day,
For beauty could begin to match
　　The fish which got away.

Perhaps against us one and all
　　Could lie the self-same charge:
The joys we catch seem very small,
　　The ones we lose seem large;
We pass our many blessings by
　　As though no worth had they,
And dolefully we magnify
　　The joy that gets away.

On Going Out

The women folks look up at me
And cry: "You are not fit to see!

That coat needs brushing, and your tie
Is old and worn and all awry
And very shabby is your hat;
Surely you won't go out like that!"

They're fretted by the speck of dirt
Which seems to settle on my shirt,
And should the collar band be worn,
Or show a spot that's frayed and torn,
They'll give the ultimatum flat:
"Now you're not going out like that!"

How easily they dust the coat
And trim the muffler round my throat!
How lightly they apply the touch
Of neatness which I need so much,
That outwardly at least I'll be
What women folks call "fit to see."

Lord, when it comes my time to die,
Let not my spirit be awry;
Grant me the time, the while I live,
To ask forgiveness and forgive,
That this old soul of mine may be,
On its arrival, "fit to see!"

Let some one come to me who knows
Where every little blemish shows
And say: "This bit of wrong, repair!
Brush off those dusty signs of care!"
And with the same old friendly pat,
Make sure I don't go out like that!

Questions for the Boy

Boy, if a mountain you should see
  Crusted with jewels thick,
And you were told that you were free
  Each day a gem to pick
And bear away the precious stone,
Henceforth to be your very own,
Would you return with spade and sack,
Or on such fortune turn your back?

Suppose by him who watched it there
  'Twas very plainly told
That each could take what he could bear
  Of silver and of gold,
But must himself alone obtain
And carry what his strength could gain,
Would you begrudge the labor which
Promised in time to make you rich?

Well, college is a mountain steep,
  With jewels richly set;
And who shall venture there may keep
  Whate'er he wills to get.
But he himself must dig it out,
Unaided carry it about,
And to that mountain come alone
To make the knowledge there his own.

Who toils for truth shall find it there—
  'Tis ever on display,

And none who watches you shall care
    How much you take away.
The gems are stored on ledge and shelf,
But you must earn them for yourself;
'Tis yours to choose and yours to say
What riches you will bear away.

Little Miss Curious

Little Miss Curious, Little Miss Pry,
Little Miss What's That and Little Miss Why,
Little Miss Tell Me and Little Miss How,
Would I could settle your problems right now,
But wait for the answers. They'll come in their turn,
And some of the things you must grow up to learn.

Little Miss Question Box, flooring me flat,
Wanting to know all of this and of that.
If when we're naughty God sees and is sad,
Why does He let little children be bad?
Why can't the angels who brought me to you
Bring me a cute little girl baby, too?

What makes the whiskers come out on your chin?
Grandma has teeth she takes out and puts in,
How did she get them, and why does she need
Glasses whenever she sits down to read?
Little Miss Busy Tongue, I can't explain
Half of the problems which trouble your brain.

Little Miss Curious, Little Miss Pry,
Little Miss What's That, and Little Miss Why,
Come with your questions and wide-open eyes,
I'll do my best, though I'm not very wise,
For even I wonder, as onward I go,
And am puzzled by things I am too young to know.

Friends Old and New

Here's to the old friends true
Who share in all we do
And have learned all our ways
Through many yesterdays.
Theirs are the hearts that share
All that we meet of care;
Theirs are the eyes that see,
Though grave our faults may be,
The good that lies below.
That's why we love them so!

But here's to the happy day
When comes across our way
A new friend, blithe and bold,
To join the faithful old.
Glad is the sheltering door
To welcome in one more.
Brighter the fireplace where
We draw another chair,
But happiest, at day's end,
Are we to gain a friend.

[174]

Old Age

I used to think that growing old was reckoned just
    in years,
But who can name the very date when weariness
    appears?
I find no stated time when man, obedient to a law,
Must settle in an easy chair and from the world with-
    draw.
Old Age is rather curious, or so it seems to me.
I know old men at forty and young men at seventy-
    three.

I'm done with counting life by years or temples
    turning gray.
No man is old who wakes with joy to greet another
    day.
What if the body cannot dance with youth's elastic
    spring?
There's many a vibrant interest to which the mind
    can cling.
'Tis in the spirit Age must dwell, or this would never
    be:
I know old men at forty and young men at seventy-
    three.

Some men keep all their friendships warm, and
    welcome friendships new,
They have no time to sit and mourn the things they
    used to do.

This changing world they greet with joy and never
	bow to fate;
On every fresh adventure they set out with hearts
	elate.
From chilling fear and bitter dread they keep their
	spirits free
While some seem old at forty they stay young at
	seventy-three.

So much to do, so much to learn, so much in which to
	share!
With twinkling eyes and minds alert some brave both
	time and care.
And this I've learned from other men, that only they
	are old
Who think with something that has passed the tale of
	life is told.
For Age is not alone of time, or we should never see
Men old and bent at forty and men young at seventy-
	three.

Brotherhood

"Am I my brother's keeper?" answered Cain
When questioned of his brother Abel, slain,
And since such record keepings first began
This phrase has lingered on the lips of man.
Still is it heard: "Oh, is it mine to care
What miseries my brother has to bear?
Lord, is it not enough that I must see
That I have food and all is well with me?"

Suppose a plague should fall upon the town,
Would it not trouble men of great renown
To learn that on some little near-by street
Were those, perhaps, they once had scorned to meet
Sore-stricken with the malady? And would
They not unite with all the neighborhood
To win to health and happiness again
The very humblest of their fellow-men?

Within their brothers' health they'd seek their own,
To them his daily progress would be known.
They'd watch the sick and suffering and share
Their misery lest the pain be theirs to bear.
For what harms one another may destroy.
Not in our own but in another's joy
Lies common welfare. Brothers are we all!
Where one man stumbles every one may fall.

Possession

When they're very, very good
And are doing as they should,
When the youngsters are polite,
Never wrong and always right,
And this very oft occurs—
Mother speaks of them as "hers."

When the parson comes for tea
Should he take them on his knee

And a blessing, soft and low,
On their little heads bestow,
In those few brief, fleeting hours,
Mother speaks of them as "ours."

But if little girl and lad
Have been very, very bad,
Have their tempers been displayed,
Have they boldly disobeyed,
Then when I come home to dine
Mother speaks of them as "mine."

Envy

I wonder if the poppy shows
The slightest envy of the rose?

Or if the pansy wastes its time
Regretting that it cannot climb?

Do blossoms of a yellow hue
Complain because they are not blue?

Do birds which God designed to sing
Envy the wild ducks' fleeter wing?

And does the sparrow sadly mourn
Because he was not goldfinch born?

I cannot say, but fancy not.
Each seems contented with his lot.

'Tis only man who thinks that he
Some other man would rather be.

If You Would Please Me

If you would please me when I've passed away
　Let not your grief embitter you. Be brave;
　Turn with full courage from my mounded grave
And smile upon the children at their play;
Let them make merry in their usual way;
　Do not with sorrow those young lives enslave
　Or steal from them the fleeting joys they crave;
Let not your grieving spoil their happy day.

Live on as you have lived these many years,
　Still let your soul be gentle and be kind—
I never liked to see those eyes in tears!
　Weep not too much that you must stay behind;
Share in the lives of others as you'd share,
If God had willed it still to leave me there.

Christmas Eve

Tomorrow morn she'll wake to see
The trinkets on her Christmas tree,
And find beside her little bed,
Where tenderly and soft of tread
Old Santa Claus has walked to leave
The toys that she might still believe.

Her stocking by the chimney place
Gives to the room a touch of grace
More beautiful than works of art
And velvet draperies can impart.
Here is a symbol of a trust
Richer than wisdom thick with dust.

I see it through the half-swung door,
And smile to think long years before
I, too, on Christmas Eve was young
And eagerly a stocking hung
Beside the chimney just as she,
Ere knowledge stole my faith from me.

Upstairs about her bed there seems
The peace of childhood's lovely dreams,
And I, grown old, almost forget
The truths with which I am beset.
Upon this blessed Christmas Eve
I, too, in Santa Claus believe.

Keep Your Dreams

Keep your dreams—they're richer far
Than the facts discovered are.

Do not seek all things to touch;
Do not want to know too much.

Growing old, still play the child;
Keep some glory undefiled.

What if clouds are mist and air?
Still see ships sailing there.

What would life be if we knew
Only those things which are true?

If the things of bad and good
Were by all men understood,

Nature's hills and brooks and springs
Would be catalogued as things.

Keep your dreams, for in them lies
Joy denied to men grown wise.

Still build castles in the air!
Still see white ships sailing there!

Still have something to pursue,
Something which you wish you knew.

Rich or Poor

The use of money marks the man.
    The wrong is not in having gold;
All men should gather what they can
    In other ways is failure told.

The sin lies not in growing rich
    But in forgetfulness of pain
And all the bitter suffering which
    Beset the men who poor remain.

No virtue lies in poverty,
    Poor men may be as vile or worse
And fail God's purpose utterly
    As those who may be rich of purse.

Within the sphere where we may dwell
    The test is not of yellow gain,
But do we use our talents well?
    Does sympathy in us remain?

'Tis not the role that makes the priest,
    'Tis not the purse that makes the man.
The proof of greatest and of least
    Is: Does he do the best he can?

The Happy Toad

As I was walking down the road
I met an ugly, grinning toad,
Who squatted in the shade and said:
"I never wish that I were dead.
Wherever I may chance to stray
I find rich food along the way;
I have no dreams I can't fulfill;
I owe no other toad a bill;
In slimy places I abide,
But with them I am satisfied.
My little children I forsook
As tadpoles in a nearby brook;
I know not where they are nor care.
I have no burdens I must bear.

At night I never lie awake.
My bitterest enemy is the snake.
I have no taxes, no beliefs,
No cares, ambitions, hopes or griefs;
No clothes to buy, no cash to lose,
No tools that I must learn to use.
I sing no dirges, tell no jokes.
I'm just a jumping toad who croaks.
Contented, placid, happy I
Shall be until the day I die."

*　　*　　*　　*

Yet, as I trudged along the road,
I thought, "Who wants to be a toad?"

The Dog

I like a dog at my feet when I read,
Whatever his size or whatever his breed.
A dog now and then that will muzzle my hand
As though I were the greatest of men in the land,
And trying to tell me it's pleasant to be
On such intimate terms with a fellow like me.

I like a dog at my side when I eat.
I like to give him a bit of my meat;
And though mother objects and insists it is bad
To let dogs in the dining room, still I am glad
To behold him stretched out on the floor by my chair.
It's cheering to see such a faithful friend there.

A dog leads a curious life at the best.
By the wag of his tail is his pleasure expressed.
He pays a high tribute to man when he stays
True to his friend to the end of his days.
And I wonder sometimes if it happens to be
That dogs pay no heed to the faults which men see.

Should I prove a failure; should I stoop to wrong;
Be weak at a time when I should have been strong,
Should I lose my money, the gossips would sneer
And fill with my blundering many an ear,
But still, as I opened my door, I should see
My dog wag his tail with a welcome for me.

"Move We Adjourn"

When I'm weary of argument wordy
　　And tired of continuous debate,
When the speaker like some hurdy gurdy,
　　Which carries on early and late,
Keeps up a monotonous bellow
　　On lessons I don't want to learn,
'Tis then I give cheers for the fellow
　　Who rises and moves to adjourn.

There are motions to lay on the table,
　　There are motions for this and for that,
And I stick just as long as I'm able
　　And hark to the chatterer's chat,

I stand for the rising thanks motion
    For the one who has done a good turn,
But my friend is the chap with the notion
    To get up and move to adjourn.

There are some who like papers and speeches,
    And open discussions of things,
The heights some new orator reaches,
    The lesson and message he brings.
But each his own fancy must cling to,
    What one chooses others may spurn,
So this simple tribute I sing to
    The brother who moves to adjourn!

Which of these popular new
Permabooks do you want?

New titles are added monthly. See your local dealer for these and other new Permabooks. If your dealer is unable to supply certain titles, send 35¢ for each book (plus 5¢ per book for postage and handling) to

PERMABOOKS
Mail Order Department
Garden City, New York